To Laura,

You're a wonderful friend to me. A huge blessing. So glad that God brought us together!

Thank you for everything. You've been more than kind to me!

Much love & appreciation,

Kristi

To _____

From _____

A CUP
OF JOY

THOMAS NELSON
Since 1798

NASHVILLE MEXICO CITY RIO DE JANEIRO

Published in Nashville, Tennessee, by Thomas Nelson. Thomas Nelson is a
registered trademark of HarperCollins Christian Publishing, Inc.

Thomas Nelson titles may be purchased in bulk for educational, business,
fund-raising, or sales promotional use. For information, please e-mail
SpecialMarkets@ThomasNelson.com.

ISBN: 978-0-7180-3916-5

Printed in China

14 15 16 17 18 DSC 6 5 4 3 2 1

May the God of hope fill you with all
joy and peace as you trust in him,
so that you may overflow with hope
by the power of the Holy Spirit.

—Romans 15:13 NIV

When you first gave your heart to God, He did a remarkable thing. He filled you with His light. He turned on the switch of His Spirit so that you would be able to recognize Him anytime you stepped out into the dark world. You are His beacon, His sunbeam. Now and then you may wonder if the light is still on or if you've allowed so much of the world to get into your heart and head that you have somehow closed the door on it. That may just mean it's time to get a jolt of direct current from the Source of all the light in the world.

You're God's moon reflecting His Son's light wherever you are. What an amazing thought! You never have to worry about whether God wants you to shine your light. You simply have to be willing to do so, and a beam will go out from you to anyone who is seeking it. You're a beacon on a hill and a welcome sight to those who wander yet in the darkness. What joy that brings!

Your Promises From God Today

· · · · · · · · · ·

You are the light of the world. A city that is
set on a hill cannot be hidden. Nor do they
light a lamp and put it under a basket, but
on a lampstand, and it gives light to all who
are in the house. Let your light so shine
before men, that they may see your good
works and glorify your Father in heaven.

MATTHEW 5:14–16

In Him was life, and the life was the light of men.

JOHN 1:4

Light is sown for the righteous,
And gladness for the upright in heart.

PSALM 97:11

Praise the LORD, call upon His name;
Declare His deeds among the peoples,
Make mention that His name is exalted.

ISAIAH 12:4

NEIGHBORS

Some of us grew up in neighborhoods. We knew most of the people who lived on our street or in the houses surrounding ours. As neighbors, we knew we could count on each other when times were tough and that we all had a lot in common.

It's not quite so easy to define neighbors today. Sure, neighborhoods still exist, but the advent of the internet has changed our definition of "neighbor" in a way that nothing before it has done. Now we realize that we have neighbors who live in other states and need our help when hurricanes and tornadoes level their homes. We see that there are children starving in countries around the globe, and there's a strong realization that we're part of a huge global family and we each have a part in that family as well. Seeds of hope need to be planted in the hearts and homes of people close to us, but at other times, our neighbors are far away.

When God reminded us to "love our neighbors," He had a wide net. Love your neighbor, offer hope to those in need, and your life will forever be rooted in joy.

Little Seeds of Hope

Behold, how good and how pleasant it is
For brethren to dwell together in unity!

Psalm 133:1

"Love your neighbor as yourself."

Matthew 19:19

"For I was hungry and you gave Me food; I
was thirsty and you gave Me drink; I was a
stranger and you took Me in; I was naked and
you clothed Me; I was sick and you visited
Me; I was in prison and you came to Me."

Matthew 25:35—36

CHARACTER
THAT HOLDS

When storms begin to blow, the integrity of a building is revealed—the strength of its foundation, the practicality of its design, and the quality of its building materials. Will it stand or will it fall?

The same holds true for your own integrity. When the pressure is on, weak spots in your faith or character readily come to light. If this happens, take note. Your integrity matures over time. If you've made unsound choices in the past, make better choices today. Make sure your foundation rests solely on what God says is true, not on what your emotions or contemporary culture says is right and fair. Then turn your face toward the wind with confidence. You and your integrity are built to last.

Living God's Way

Keep my soul, and deliver me;
Let me not be ashamed, for I put my trust in You.
Let integrity and uprightness preserve me,
For I wait for You.

PSALM 25:20—21

"The Helper, the Holy Spirit, whom the Father
will send in My name, He will teach you all
things, and bring to your remembrance all
things that I said to you. Peace I leave with
you, My peace I give to you; not as the world
gives do I give to you. Let not your heart
be troubled, neither let it be afraid."

JOHN 14:26—27

He who walks with integrity walks securely,
But he who perverts his ways will become known.

PROVERBS 10:9

LET GOD TAKE
THE CREDIT

As you anticipate an exciting new chapter in your life, remember: The coming chapter, like every other, begins and ends with God and with His Son.

God will touch your heart and guide your steps—if you let Him. So dedicate this day to God's purpose and give thanks for His grace. Take a minute to write a note of thanks to God, celebrating the good things about your life right now and in the future, and expressing your gratitude. Tuck the note in your Bible or journal so you can look back at it often.

This is the day the Lord has created—give thanks to the One who created it, and use it to the glory of His kingdom.

Living God's Way

For the LORD God is a sun and shield;
The LORD will give grace and glory;
No good thing will He withhold
From those who walk uprightly.

PSALM 84:11

He who did not spare His own Son, but
delivered Him up for us all, how shall He not
with Him also freely give us all things?

ROMANS 8:32

Whatever you do in word or deed, do all
in the name of the Lord Jesus, giving
thanks to God the Father through Him.

COLOSSIANS 3:17

UNPLUG

I'm thinking that God didn't rest after Creation because it really tuckered Him out. He merely spoke and things came to be. No, God knew that if He didn't model rest for us, we wouldn't get it. So He did. He worked, and then He rested.

For many of us, resting does not come easily. We feel unworthy if we are not pulling our weight. But any farmer worth his salt knows that you can't plow with the same oxen more than six hours at a time. The beasts need rest. The farmer also knows that if you continue to plant a field season after season and never allow it to go fallow and replenish its nutrients, the harvest will be weak. . . .

It is difficult for us to admit that we need it, but a once-a-week "unplugging" from the frenetic pace that is now our norm can be one of the most spiritually liberating experiences for us and for our family.

ANITA RENFROE

The Purse-Driven Life

. . . .

"Work shall be done for six days, but the seventh
is the Sabbath of rest, holy to the LORD."

EXODUS 31:15

Rest in the LORD, and wait patiently for Him.

PSALM 37:7

"This Book of the Law shall not depart
from your mouth, but you shall meditate
in it day and night, that you may observe to
do according to all that is written in it. For
then you will make your way prosperous,
and then you will have good success."

JOSHUA 1:8

GOD IS IN CONTROL

One morning my computer simply would not obey me. What a nuisance. I had my work laid out, my timing figured, my mind all set. My work was delayed, my timing thrown off, my thinking interrupted. Then I remembered. It was not for nothing. This was part of the Plan (not mine, His). "Lord, You have assigned me my portion and my cup."

Now if the interruption had been a human being instead of an infuriating mechanism, it would not have been so hard to see it as the most important part of the work of the day. But all is under my Father's control: yes, recalcitrant computers, faulty transmissions, drawbridges which happen to be up when one is in a hurry. My portion. My cup. My lot is secure. My heart can be at peace. My Father is in charge. How simple!

ELISABETH ELLIOT

Keep a Quiet Heart

Be anxious for nothing, but in everything by
prayer and supplication, with thanksgiving,
let your requests be made known to God;
and the peace of God, which surpasses all
understanding, will guard your hearts
and minds through Christ Jesus.

PHILIPPIANS 4:6–7

Whom have I in heaven but You?
And there is none upon earth
that I desire besides You.
My flesh and my heart fail;
But God is the strength of my heart
and my portion forever.

PSALM 73:25–26

Rejoice always, pray without ceasing, in
everything give thanks; for this is the
will of God in Christ Jesus for you.

1 THESSALONIANS 5:16–18

A TOXIN CLEANSE
FOR THE SOUL

Little did I know how very spiritual the fast [my "toxin cleanse" of twenty-one days] would become. . . . Without the distraction of frappuccinos and French fries, I quickly realized there were more toxins clogging my *soul* than there were triglycerides clogging my arteries. The extra weight I was carrying in my spirit was much more dangerous than the fluff I was carrying around my hips and waist. . . .

For the moment my heart feels significantly lighter. It's not weighed down by emotional fatty deposits like, *Why do I always have to be the one who says "I'm sorry" first?* . . . Or *If God isn't going to give me a husband and children, why doesn't He at least bless me with a best-selling book and a high metabolism?* Today—well, at least this morning—those kinds of toxic thoughts that sometimes clog my soul are gone. I am fasting from whiny narcissism and a sense of entitlement. Right now I'm content just being a sturdy, mistake-prone girl who is absolutely adored by a perfect Redeemer!

LISA HARPER

Stumbling into Grace

Who can discern their own errors?
Forgive my hidden faults.
Keep your servant also from willful sins;
may they not rule over me.
Then I will be blameless,
innocent of great transgression.

PSALM 19:12–13 NIV

The good that I will to do, I do not do; but
the evil I will not to do, that I practice.

ROMANS 7:19

Whatever things are true, whatever things
are noble, whatever things are just, whatever
things are pure, whatever things are lovely,
whatever things are of good report, if
there is any virtue and if there is anything
praiseworthy—meditate on these things.

PHILIPPIANS 4:8

YOUR PASSION AND
YOUR PURPOSE

You are here for a reason. There is nothing accidental about you. There is a specific purpose, assignment, and mission on earth that only you can fulfill. Never doubt your specialness. Even on days when you can't see an end in sight and the light at the end of the tunnel seems more like a faint spark, press on through the dark. Trust in your destiny. It is calling you, beckoning you, waiting for you . . . even when you can't yet see it.

Your identity was decided long before you were ever born by a God who is daily placing new desires and hopes and dreams into your heart. Your heart is the foundation of everything that makes you *you* and is the clearest signal you'll ever receive about your destiny, your purpose, your calling. To identify who you are, you must first identify what you love. . . .

When you step back and gaze upon where your passion and your personality intersect, therein lies your purpose.

MANDY HALE

The Single Woman

· · · · · · · · ·

My frame was not hidden from You,
When I was made in secret,
And skillfully wrought in the
lowest parts of the earth.
Your eyes saw my substance, being yet unformed.
And in Your book they all were written,
The days fashioned for me,
When as yet there were none of them.

PSALM 139:15—16

I heard the voice of the Lord, saying:
"Whom shall I send,
And who will go for Us?"
Then I said, "Here am I! Send me."

ISAIAH 6:8

Take great joy in the Eternal!
His gifts are coming, and they
are all your heart desires!

PSALM 37:4 THE VOICE

RECEIVING GOD'S
HARD LESSONS

Each time God gives us a hard lesson, He desires also to give us Himself. If we open our hands to receive the lesson we open our hearts to receive Him, and with Himself His vision to see the glory in the surrender, whether of small things like self-esteem and reputation, or bigger things like a career and a home. He has been over the trail first, for He surrendered His glory, His equality with the Father, His omnipotence, His omnipresence, His all, when He came into our world. He stands ready today to supply us with His wisdom to understand what He wants to teach, and His strength to carry through, for He never allows us to undergo anything for which He has not promised the strength to endure. His commands are always accompanied by power to obey.

ELISABETH ELLIOT

A Path Through Suffering

Scarcely for a righteous man will one die;
yet perhaps for a good man someone would
even dare to die. But God demonstrates
His own love toward us, in that while we
were still sinners, Christ died for us.

ROMANS 5:7—8

"Be strong and of good courage; do not
be afraid, nor be dismayed, for the LORD
your God is with you wherever you go."

JOSHUA 1:9

Hear my cry, O God;
Attend to my prayer.
From the end of the earth I will cry to You,
When my heart is overwhelmed;
Lead me to the rock that is higher than I.

PSALM 61:1—2

SEEKING
SHELTER IN GOD

Some Christians treat God as a kind of insurance agent. In hard times, they expect Him to issue a claim check to restore what they've lost. While waiting for Him to change their circumstances for the better, they withhold fellowship from Him. Life's "squeeze" reveals their lack of submission and stubborn attitudes.

It is the heaven-born instinct of a child of God to seek shelter beneath the wings of the Almighty. The tendency to complain or to assert that God owes us something is not spiritual.

The godly instinct of a child of God is to say with Job, "Oh, that I might find Him."

JONI EARECKSON TADA

Seeking God

Keep me as the apple of Your eye;
Hide me under the shadow of Your wings.

PSALM 17:8

You have been a shelter for me,
A strong tower from the enemy.
I will abide in Your tabernacle forever;
I will trust in the shelter of Your wings.

PSALM 61:3–4

Deliver me, O LORD, from my enemies;
In You I take shelter.
Teach me to do Your will,
For You are my God.

PSALM 143:9–10

NEED A REST?

Do you ever just get tired of trying? It feels like you've prayed and you've tried a lot of things, but nothing seems to change. You start to wonder if you have some kind of black cloud that just hangs over your head. Maybe you're just tired. Maybe it's time to give yourself a break and take a little rest. After all, even Jesus enjoyed a good nap now and then.

Put your head on God's shoulder and relax a bit. Some days all you need is a chance to stop the noise and the chaos of all that is going on around you and simply rest. God invites you in. He knows you need a break and is happy to spend some quiet time just with you.

Your Promises from God Today

. . . .

"Come to Me, all you who labor and are heavy
laden, and I will give you rest. Take My yoke upon
you and learn from Me, for I am gentle and lowly
in heart, and you will find rest for your souls."

MATTHEW 11:28–29

Be anxious for nothing, but in everything by
prayer and supplication, with thanksgiving,
let your requests be made known to God;
and the peace of God, which surpasses all
understanding, will guard your hearts
and minds through Christ Jesus.

PHILIPPIANS 4:6–7

He gives power to the weak,
And to those who have no might
He increases strength.
Even the youths shall faint and be weary,
And the young men shall utterly fall.

ISAIAH 40:29–30

FOCUSING ON GOD

Prayer is not merely going to God with a shopping list of things we want Him to do for us and for our families. Rather, it is being in relationship with Him, listening to Him, and sharing our hearts with Him. . . .

We must remember who it is that we are talking with—the Almighty God. I have found it helpful to begin and end my prayers by focusing on His character traits. He is the Almighty God. He is the God who heals. He is the God of peace. He is the God who forgives. He is the God who provides, and He is the God who is in control. He knows everything that is happening. He is not caught off guard. His love is perfect.

As I consider who He is instead of focusing on myself or another person or my situation, I am better able to pray with faith.

SUSAN ALEXANDER YATES

A House Full of Friends

. . . .

"In returning and rest you shall be saved;
In quietness and confidence
shall be your strength."

ISAIAH 30:15

The works of the LORD are great,
Studied by all who have pleasure in them.
His work is honorable and glorious,
And His righteousness endures forever.
He has made His wonderful works
to be remembered;
The LORD is gracious and full of compassion.

PSALM 111:2—4

So we are always confident, knowing that while
we are at home in the body we are absent from
the Lord. For we walk by faith, not by sight.

2 CORINTHIANS 5:6—7

THE SECRET OF JOY

What secret do believers filled with joy know? They practice the presence of God. Remember the euphoria you had as a new believer? How amazed you were to discover that the God who made the universe loved you and might intervene personally in your day? You were on the right track then, but so often as time passes we lose that sense of anticipation. We lose the glow.

Run after God the way you did when you first fell in love. Wake up talking to Him, thanking Him for the hot shower, the fragrance of coffee. Ask Him for direction for your day. Expect Him to speak to you from His Word. Watch for Him in the people who cross your path—yes, even in the interruptions. Talk with Him in the night. Set the Lord always before you, and He will fill you with joy and with pleasures forevermore.

DEE BRESTIN

Women of Faith Devotional Bible

······· ··

You will show me the path of life;
In Your presence is fullness of joy;
At Your right hand are pleasures forevermore.

PSALM 16:11

"Are not two sparrows sold for a copper coin?
And not one of them falls to the ground apart
from your Father's will. But the very hairs of your
head are all numbered. Do not fear therefore;
you are of more value than many sparrows."

MATTHEW 10:29–31

Your words were found, and I ate them,
And Your word was to me the joy
and rejoicing of my heart.

JEREMIAH 15:16

THINK YES!

When we get up in the morning, we have just so much energy. We can spend that energy creatively, seeking positive solutions, or we can spend it dragging ourselves down with negative thinking. Either way, we may still be tired at the end of the day. But in the first instance, we will have accomplished something and made progress. In the other we will have plodded along and managed to make ourselves not only tired, but depressed as well!

Half the battle in solving problems is our attitude. We are not just pumping ourselves full of sunshine when we say, "Think YES!" How we think about a situation usually dictates the course we will take. And sometimes, when we get bogged down in all the tangle of detail, we need a friend who will help us think clearly about all aspects of the situation, refocusing our attention from the obstacles to the possibilities in striving for proper choices and desired goals.

GLORIA GAITHER

Decisions

The LORD is for me among those who help me. . . .
It is better to trust in the LORD
Than to put confidence in man.
It is better to trust in the LORD
Than to put confidence in princes.

PSALM 118:7–9

Listen to counsel and receive instruction,
That you may be wise in your latter days.

PROVERBS 19:20

The righteous and the wise and their
works are in the hand of God.

ECCLESIASTES 9:1

A LESSON FROM
THE ORCHESTRA

An orchestra, to be worthy of its name, is like love. It demands *doing* as well as *feeling*.

And it *takes practice, practice,* PRACTICE. Its members may not feel like correcting the mistakes, but they do—until the problem is resolved. They may not feel that they can endure going over and over the areas in which they continue to make mistakes, but they do—until they can communicate, share, and encourage the other members in spite of the difficulties. Only then can they become a "whole." . . .

Each instrument occupies a special "chair." Each adds a unique movement. Yet each must retain its individual beauty. And oh, how fine-tuned each instrument must be! . . .

We form an orchestra, too. Each of us is an integral part of the whole with our families, coworkers, friends. . . . To create a symphony, we must keep our ears tuned to one another, our eyes focused on the Director.

JUNE MASTERS BACHER

The Quiet Heart

Comfort each other and edify one
another, just as you also are doing. . . .
Be at peace among yourselves.

1 Thessalonians 5:11, 13

"I will be a Father to you,
And you shall be My sons and daughters,
Says the Lord Almighty."

2 Corinthians 6:18

As each one has received a gift, minister
it to one another, as good stewards
of the manifold grace of God.

1 Peter 4:10

STRENGTHENING
YOUR MARRIAGE

God requires the husband to *love* his wife, but the wife is required to have *respect* for her husband. I assume no woman would marry a man she didn't love, but too often a wife loses respect for her husband after they've been married awhile. Loss of respect seems to precede loss of love and is more hurtful to a man than we realize. . . .

If this has already happened to you, and you know you've shown disrespect for your husband, confess it to God right now. Say, "Lord, I confess I do not esteem my husband the way Your Word says to. There is a wall in my heart that I know was erected as a protection against being hurt. But I am ready to let it come down so that my heart can heal." . . .

Praying like this will free you to see your man's potential for greatness as opposed to his flaws. It will enable you to say something positive that will encourage, build up, give life, and make the marriage better.

STORMIE OMARTIAN

The Power of a Praying Wife

Let each one of you in particular so love
his own wife as himself, and let the wife
see that she respects her husband.

EPHESIANS 5:33

[Let] older women . . . be reverent in
behavior, not slanderers, not given to
much wine, teachers of good things—that
they admonish the young women to love
their husbands, to love their children.

TITUS 2:3—4

An excellent wife is the crown of her husband.

PROVERBS 12:4

GOD REJOICES IN YOU!

What brings God great joy and genuine pleasure? His people! He delights in those who have pledged their loyalty to Him and recognize His position as Almighty God, Author of history, Deliverer, Redeemer, and King. He delights in those people who acknowledge Jesus as their Savior and then choose to serve Him as their Lord. Further delight comes when His people obey Him and when they persevere in their faith during tough and challenging days.

Consider again the wonderful promises of Zephaniah 3:17. This Mighty [God] will save: He will bring peace, redemption, guidance, and hope to any and every situation you, His child, find yourself in. When you choose to walk in obedience to Him, He will rejoice over you with gladness and song. He will also come alongside to quiet you with His love when circumstances call for that.

The Lord your God is a God of joy. Know that He rejoices in you!

100 Favorite Bible Verses

The LORD your God in your midst,
The Mighty One, will save;
He will rejoice over you with gladness,
He will quiet you with His love,
He will rejoice over you with singing.

ZEPHANIAH 3:17

The LORD was my support.
He also brought me out into a broad place;
He delivered me because He delighted in me.

PSALM 18:18—19

Jesus [is] the author and finisher of our faith,
who for the joy that was set before Him endured
the cross, despising the shame, and has sat
down at the right hand of the throne of God.

HEBREWS 12:2

BECOME A HIT

Most people suffer from chronic performance anxiety. Is that the case with you? Are you constantly wondering what kind of reviews you will receive from your family, your boss, or your coworkers? If so, here's a little stage wisdom to help you cope.

Kill the foot lights and turn up the house lights. When you do, you will see that there is only one VIP in the audience—God. Ultimately, His review is the only one that matters. Live your life in a manner that is pleasing to Him. Doing so will build your confidence because you will be establishing your life on something solid instead of on the shifting sands of people's opinions. So, chase away your anxiety and live your life for God. You're bound to be a hit with Him.

Living God's Way

Be diligent to present yourself approved
to God, a worker who does not need to be
ashamed, rightly dividing the word of truth.

2 TIMOTHY 2:15

I am persuaded that neither death nor life,
nor angels nor principalities nor powers,
nor things present nor things to come, nor
height nor depth, nor any other created thing,
shall be able to separate us from the love of
God which is in Christ Jesus our Lord.

ROMANS 8:38—39

"His lord said to him, 'Well done,
good and faithful servant.'"

MATTHEW 25:21

AN ACQUIRED TASTE

Will I ever be content? . . . Yes. It's something I have to choose daily. I know there will be moments when I'll get a bee in my bonnet about replacing our countertops or I'll grumble because I have white appliances and not stainless steel. In those times, I have to stop focusing on everything I want and focus on what I have. I'm not saying that getting to a place of complete contentment is easy, but I know that I am much happier (and so is my family) when I'm not consumed with my wish list.

If you've struggled to find contentment as I have, you don't have to wallow in your past shortcomings. We've all had those moments when we're in a funk because we feel like we should have hardwood floors instead of the beige carpet the previous owners installed that is now spotted with stains. . . . But even on bad days with bad carpet, we can set our sights on the things that really matter—such as friendship, family, and faith—and live our lives with a spirit of contentment.

MARIAN PARSONS

Inspired You

········

I have learned in whatever state
I am, to be content.

PHILIPPIANS 4:11

Godliness with contentment is great gain.
For we brought nothing into this world, and
it is certain we can carry nothing out.

1 TIMOTHY 6:6—7

Let your conduct be without covetousness;
be content with such things as you
have. For He Himself has said, "I will
never leave you nor forsake you."

HEBREWS 13:5

GAZE AT THE LORD

The dog has tracked Alpo all over the kitchen floor. Your husband has called to say he'll be late. The saucepans are boiling over, and the burning casserole is staining your oven. Teenagers are wrestling in the bedroom above your kitchen. Little wonder you stand there with the dish towel in your hand, droop-shouldered and dumbfounded, not knowing what to do.

What we need here is more than a prayer mumbled in obligation. . . . We need a different focus. . . .

Consider Jesus. He had one heavy cross to bear, but He fixed His sight on the joy before Him. And we are to do the same.

So what about the burning casserole, the dirty kitchen floor, and the screaming kids upstairs? They haven't changed. But your focus has. Don't gaze at your problems while you only glance at the Lord. Get life in focus. Gaze at the Lord—behold Him—and your problems won't cause you to grow weary and lose heart.

JONI EARECKSON TADA

Seeking God

· · · · · · · · · ·

Let us run with endurance the race that is
set before us, looking unto Jesus, the author
and finisher of our faith, who for the joy
that was set before Him endured the cross,
despising the shame, and has sat down at
the right hand of the throne of God.

HEBREWS 12:1–2

One thing I have desired of the LORD,
That will I seek:
That I may dwell in the house of the LORD
All the days of my life,
To behold the beauty of the LORD.

PSALM 27:4

Who among all these does not know
That the hand of the LORD has done this,
In whose hand is the life of every living thing,
And the breath of all mankind?

JOB 12:9–10

STOP LOOKING
FOR THE *WHY*

Sometimes it's a job, an opportunity, or a dream—the thing we wanted so badly . . . and prayed for [that] goes up in smoke. Sometimes we get fired when we've been model employees. Sometimes a person we have loved and invested our time, energy, affection, and trust in walks away and leaves us in the dust with little to no explanation. . . .

Stop trying to solve the mystery. . . . Stop looking for the *why* and start looking for the *good* in good-bye—because it's there. . . . The exit of that person, thing, or dream was a boarding pass to somewhere new, somewhere better, somewhere you need to be that you weren't going to reach without losing some of the baggage. Realize that if a door closed, it's because what was behind it wasn't meant for you.

Every time you release your hold on what is old, you issue an invitation to God to fill up that space with something new. The place you were might've been great, but it can't hold a candle to where you can go.

MANDY HALE

The Single Woman

. . . .

"My thoughts are not your thoughts,
Nor are your ways My ways," says the LORD.
"For as the heavens are higher than the earth,
So are My ways higher than your ways,
And My thoughts than your thoughts."

ISAIAH 55:8—9

You number my wanderings;
Put my tears into Your bottle;
Are they not in Your book?
When I cry out to You,
Then my enemies will turn back;
This I know, because God is for me.

PSALM 56:8—9

In God I have put my trust;
I will not be afraid.
What can man do to me?

PSALM 56:11

FINDING JOY IN
YOUR WORK

Work should always be associated with joy. . . .

The story is told of three women washing clothes. A passerby asked each what she was doing.

"Washing clothes" was the first answer.

"A bit of household drudgery" was the second.

"I'm mothering three young children who someday will fill important and useful spheres in life, and wash-day is a part of my grand task in caring for these souls who shall live forever" was the third.

Ordinary work, which is what most of us do most of the time, is ordained by God every bit as much as is the extraordinary. All work done for God is spiritual work and therefore not merely a duty but a holy privilege.

ELISABETH ELLIOT

The Shaping of a Christian Family

Whatever you do, do it heartily, as
to the Lord and not to men.

COLOSSIANS 3:23

I can do all things through Christ
who strengthens me.

PHILIPPIANS 4:13

In all labor there is profit.

PROVERBS 14:23

The LORD will give strength to His people;
The LORD will bless His people with peace.

PSALM 29:11

ADOPTION INTO
GOD'S FAMILY

As Christians, we are adopted as God's children. To change metaphors, we are grafted into the Vine. This process begins when we enter into relationship with Christ; we immediately benefit from becoming part of His family.

In telling the parable of the vine and the branches, Jesus explained, "I am the vine; you are the branches. Whoever abides in me and I in him, he it is that bears much fruit, for apart from me you can do nothing" (John 15:5).

When we abide in Jesus, we start taking on characteristics of His life flowing through us—the inward evidence of His influence and the indwelling work of His Spirit. The "fruit" Jesus spoke of is the outward change that comes as a result of adoption into His family.

We who are followers of Christ receive many benefits when we choose to live aligned with Jesus' goodness and righteousness. Our Lord's desires become our desires; His plans for us become plans of our own. We are shaped—reshaped—by Him as we allow His influence into every area of our lives.

A Jane Austen Devotional

"Abide in Me, and I in you. As the branch cannot bear fruit of itself, unless it abides in the vine, neither can you, unless you abide in Me."

JOHN 15:4

Behold what manner of love the Father has bestowed on us, that we should be called children of God!

1 JOHN 3:1

You received the Spirit of adoption by whom we cry out, "Abba, Father." The Spirit Himself bears witness with our spirit that we are children of God.

ROMANS 8:15—16

Years ago, I read that the average woman today has the equivalent of *fifty* full-time servants, in the form of modern, timesaving devices and equipment. That figure may or may not be accurate, but we certainly have many conveniences available to us that were unknown to women of past generations. Imagine going back to the days when there were no dishwashers, microwaves, washing machines, dryers, or automobiles. . . .

So why are our lives more harried and hurried than ever? Why are we so stressed out? . . .

In Jesus' words, we find a clue—a powerful Truth that sets us free from the bondage of hurry and frustration about all we have to do. Notice what work Jesus completed in the thirty-three years He was here on the earth: "I have finished the work *which thou gavest me to do*" (John 17:4 KJV). That is the secret. Jesus didn't finish everything His disciples wanted Him to do. . . . He didn't finish everything the multitudes wanted Him to do. . . . But He did finish the work that *God* gave Him to do.

NANCY LEIGH DEMOSS

Lies Women Believe

As for me and my house, we will serve the LORD.

JOSHUA 24:15

Six days you shall labor and do all your work,
but the seventh day is the Sabbath of the LORD
your God. In it you shall do no work. . . . For
in six days the LORD made the heavens and
the earth, the sea, and all that is in them, and
rested the seventh day. Therefore the LORD
blessed the Sabbath day and hallowed it.

EXODUS 20:9–11

A woman who fears the LORD,
she shall be praised. . . .
And let her own works praise her in the gates.

PROVERBS 31:30–31

SIN—FORGIVEN
AND FORGOTTEN

It's been said that there is only one thing God cannot do, and that is to remember your sin and mine that has been forgiven. When I come to Him humbly, through faith in Jesus, He erases my sin from His memory much more effectively than I erase things from my computer. Even Satan can't retrieve it from the inner workings of my spiritual hard drive!

Corrie ten Boom, author of *The Hiding Place* and survivor of the Nazi concentration camps during World War II, once remarked that God has cast our sins into the depths of the sea and posted a sign that says, "No Fishing Allowed."

ANNE GRAHAM LOTZ

I Saw the Lord

For as the heavens are high above the earth,
So great is His mercy toward those who fear Him;
As far as the east is from the west,
So far has He removed our
transgressions from us.
As a father pities his children,
So the LORD pities those who fear Him.

PSALM 103:11—13

In Him we have redemption through
His blood, the forgiveness of sins,
according to the riches of His grace.

EPHESIANS 1:7

If we walk in the light as He is in the light, we
have fellowship with one another, and the blood
of Jesus Christ His Son cleanses us from all sin.

1 JOHN 1:7

A MATTER OF
PERSPECTIVE

No one could convince you that black is white or up is down. But Paul does a good job of making a case that heavy is light.

A burden is heavy when its presence is pointless, when traveling with it is lonely, and when the journey is long. But life's afflictions are purposeful, not pointless. God uses our hardships to make us more like Jesus.

Furthermore we need not travel alone during this lifelong process of transformation. Fellow believers have their own afflictions, and we can be physical reminders that God is sovereign.

Finally, walking with fellow believers can help us keep focused on the unseen and eternal reward that God has for His people.

Trust in God's sovereign goodness, walk with His people, and remind yourself that the unseen and eternal are far more important than the seen and temporary. Life's afflictions will then be lighter.

100 Favorite Bible Verses

Our light affliction, which is but for a
moment, is working for us a far more
exceeding and eternal weight of glory, while
we do not look at the things which are seen,
but at the things which are not seen.

2 Corinthians 4:17—18

Bear one another's burdens, and so
fulfill the law of Christ. For if anyone
thinks himself to be something, when
he is nothing, he deceives himself.

Galatians 6:2—3

Two are better than one,
Because they have a good reward for their labor.
For if they fall, one will lift up his companion.
But woe to him who is alone when he falls,
For he has no one to help him up.

Ecclesiastes 4:9—10

REST—AND
APPRECIATE LIFE!

Some of you will appreciate my newfound area of excellence: doing nothing and resting afterward. It flies in the face of the Puritan work ethic we've all been taught and feels more decadent than a five-pound box of Godiva chocolates all to yourself. I would love to start a new habit amongst us perpetually tired women: ritualized resting.

Doesn't it seem that Sunday afternoons were specially made for napping? . . . I've always felt cheated that we live in a country that doesn't embrace the afternoon siesta. . . .

I love that the Bible tells us God didn't create Sabbath for Himself but that it was a life principle we human beings were desperately in need of. It seems that one of the most difficult things to do is to truly cease from all of our efforts and then relax and enjoy our life apart from the work of it. . . . I challenge you to start taking a day once a week to truly rest and appreciate the life God has given you.

ANITA RENFROE

The Purse-Driven Life

· · · · · · · · · ·

"Come to Me, all you who labor and are
heavy laden, and I will give you rest."

Remember the Sabbath day, to keep it holy.

"In six days the Lord made the heavens and
the earth, the sea, and all that is in them, and
rested the seventh day. Therefore the Lord
blessed the Sabbath day and hallowed it."

Happily ever after has a wonderful ring to it, and many people do their best to try to secure that happy ending. They have their rabbit's foot, their lucky hat, or their not-to-be-varied pregame routine. Some of us Christians don't worry about having a rabbit's foot, but we do grab onto Romans 8:28 as something of a good luck charm.

But is this verse truly a happily-ever-after promise? God works for the good of those who love Him (criterion #1) and whom He has called according to His purpose for them (criterion #2). Verse 29 explains that purpose: God wants His people to become more like Jesus.

Jesus is sinless, holy, and pure. Jesus is patient and kind; He is not envious, boastful, rude, self-centered, irritable, or evil thinking.

God uses every event, relationship, challenge, and hurt that we experience to make us more like Jesus. No one can improve on that happily ever after.

100 Favorite Bible Verses

. . . .

All things work together for good to those
who love God, to those who are the called
according to His purpose. For whom He
foreknew, He also predestined to be conformed
to the image of His Son, that He might be
the firstborn among many brethren.

ROMANS 8:28–29

You are a chosen generation, a royal priesthood,
a holy nation, His own special people, that
you may proclaim the praises of Him who
called you out of darkness into His marvelous
light; who once were not a people but are
now the people of God, who had not obtained
mercy but now have obtained mercy.

1 PETER 2:9–10

"You are the light of the world. . . . Let your light
so shine before men, that they may see your
good works and glorify your Father in heaven."

MATTHEW 5:14, 16

POURING GOD'S
GRACE ON OTHERS

We human beings have an overwhelming tendency to jump to conclusions, to expect the worst in order to avoid disappointment, and to turn our backs on people who hurt us. Yet the Bible says, "Love never gives up, never loses faith, is always hopeful, and endures through every circumstance" (1 Corinthians 13:7 NLT).

The extent to which we are able to demonstrate this kind of love requires God's operative grace in our lives. We can love with this kind of love when we remember that life is *not about us*; it's about dying to self and surrendering our sinful tendencies to Christ. When we do, we are freed up to love one another as we want to be loved ourselves, and we get a taste of how we are loved by Christ.

Think about whom you struggle most to love. Pray about that relationship, surrender it to Christ, and begin letting His love flow through you to other imperfect humans.

A Jane Austen Devotional

"A new commandment I give to you, that
you love one another; as I have loved
you, that you also love one another."

JOHN 13:34

Let nothing be done through selfish ambition
or conceit, but in lowliness of mind let each
esteem others better than himself. Let each
of you look out not only for his own interests,
but also for the interests of others.

PHILIPPIANS 2:3–4

"Whoever desires to become great among
you shall be your servant. And whoever of
you desires to be first shall be slave of all."

MARK 10:43–44

FIGHT FOR LOVE

Throughout history, there have been heroes and warriors of every nation and creed, but no one fought harder for love—and won—than Jesus Christ.

Even when it became deadly for Him to love rebellious, self-centered, and hateful people, Jesus never quit. He fought, died, and rose again—because of love. But it wasn't just any love. It was a higher love—an absurd, illogical, crazy love not common to this world.

It's that kind of love we're going for. Bring that love to mind when you are tempted to give up on a difficult person, relationship, job, church, or calling.

Pursue love. Make love a habit. Fight to see it rise again.

More Than a Bucket List

God demonstrates His own love toward us, in that
while we were still sinners, Christ died for us.

ROMANS 5:8

By this we know love, because He
laid down His life for us.

1 JOHN 3:16

In this is love, not that we loved God, but
that He loved us and sent His Son to be the
propitiation for our sins. Beloved, if God so
loved us, we also ought to love one another.

1 JOHN 4:10–11

THE FRAGRANT
KNOWLEDGE OF GOD

I love crisp, cold days when you can smell the smoke of a cherry-wood fire from a neighbor's chimney. . . . I love the smell of fresh, damp laundry that you hang outside on the line. . . .

In 2 Corinthians 2:14 Paul wrote, "But thanks be to God, who always leads us in triumphal procession in Christ and through us spreads everywhere the fragrance of the knowledge of him."

That idea was borrowed from the ancient Roman parades of triumph. The apostle Paul compared himself, first, to one of the prisoners led in long chains behind the conqueror's chariot; then, to a servant bearing incense; and lastly, to the incense itself that rose all along the procession of triumph.

Paul knew the power behind a sweet fragrance. It is as though he were saying, . . . "I want my words and deeds to bring to the mind of God those wonderful, similar memories of the earthly life of Jesus."

JONI EARECKSON TADA

Seeking God

Let your heart therefore be loyal to the
LORD our God, to walk in His statutes and
keep His commandments, as at this day.

1 KINGS 8:61

Let us not grow weary while doing good, for in
due season we shall reap if we do not lose heart.

GALATIANS 6:9

Be doers of the word, and not hearers
only, deceiving yourselves.

JAMES 1:22

REAL STRENGTH

We have all known women who were strong, but not very honorable. Our television screens [and movies] are filled with them. And there are women who are honorable, but frankly, not very strong. The first setback or the first perceived threat, and they fold up like a card table.

The kind of women most of us long to be are both strong and honorable, clothed with the kind of power that comes from on high, certain of our value in God's eyes, definite in our calling, and moving forward with complete assurance. Francis De Sales said, "Nothing is so strong as gentleness, nothing so gentle as real strength."

LIZ CURTIS HIGGS

Only Angels Can Wing It

· · · · · · · · · ·

Let your gentleness be known to all men.

PHILIPPIANS 4:5

"Be strong and of good courage; do not
be afraid, nor be dismayed, for the LORD
your God is with you wherever you go."

JOSHUA 1:9

In you, O LORD, I put my trust;
Let me never be put to shame.
Deliver me in Your righteousness,
and cause me to escape;
Incline Your ear to me, and save me. . . .
For You are my hope, O Lord GOD,
You are my trust from my youth.

PSALM 71:1—2, 5

AN ANCHOR
THROUGH CHANGE

Spinning! Spiraling! Up! Down! Round and round! Nothing seems to stay the same. As soon as you're comfortable, things change. If it feels like things are moving too fast for you these days, you may have to work at slowing the pace. Being intentional about finding a few quiet moments to let the world simply go by is a good thing. The One who made order out of chaos is still in control.

Change often makes fear into an ally. Fear likes to remind you that you're out of your comfort zone. It heckles you about why things can't stay the same. The other voice of change is opportunity. It gives you a chance to stop and look at where you've been and where you want to go. Go to God! He's the same yesterday, today, and forever!

Memorize one of these scriptures. Write it on a note card, and repeat it several times a day until it really moves from your head to your heart. Let it echo in your mind every time you become anxious about life. Give yourself a moment to breathe in the small, still voice of God.

Your Promises from God Today

Of old You laid the foundation of the earth,
And the heavens are the work of Your hands.
They will perish, but You will endure;
Yes, they will all grow old like a garment;
Like a cloak You will change them,
And they will be changed.
But You are the same,
And Your years will have no end.

PSALM 102:25—27

Be still, and know that I am God;
I will be exalted among the nations,
I will be exalted in the earth!
The LORD of hosts is with us;
The God of Jacob is our refuge.

PSALM 46:10—11

And the LORD, He is the One who goes before
you. He will be with you, He will not leave you
nor forsake you; do not fear nor be dismayed.

DEUTERONOMY 31:8

True knowledge of Christ comes only as we are willing to give up our dreams of glory, praying to be identified with Him on the cross. . . . Are we really willing to let God take us through times of defeat and despair, when we experience communion with Him in His crucifixion?

The wonder of God's goodness is that He can use these "crosses" for our sanctification, just as He used the death of Jesus to advance His redemptive plan. "You meant evil against me, but God meant it for good," Joseph told his brothers (Genesis 50:20). Christians sometimes think it a matter of piety to deny the evil done to them—to cover it up, say it wasn't so bad, wear a smile in public.

Yet Joseph did not shrink from calling his brothers' actions evil, and neither should we. In this world, we too will be rejected by people with sinful motives, and for the sake of truth we should call it what it is. But we can also turn it to good by realizing that suffering gives us a chance to enter spiritually upon the journey that Jesus mapped out for us: rejected, slain (spiritually), and, finally, raised.

NANCY PEARCEY

Total Truth

We also glory in tribulations, knowing that
tribulation produces perseverance; and
perseverance, character; and character, hope.
Now hope does not disappoint, because the
love of God has been poured out in our hearts
by the Holy Spirit who was given to us.

ROMANS 5:3—5

"If anyone desires to come after Me,
let him deny himself, and take up
his cross daily, and follow Me."

LUKE 9:23

We do not lose heart. Though outwardly we are
wasting away, yet inwardly we are being renewed
day by day. For our light and momentary troubles
are achieving for us an eternal glory that far
outweighs them all. So we fix our eyes not on
what is seen, but on what is unseen, since what is
seen is temporary, but what is unseen is eternal.

2 CORINTHIANS 4:16—18 NIV

GOD SHOWS US
WHAT IS GOOD

God's most powerful illustration of what is good is His own Son. Jesus overturned the tables of the money changers who had made His Father's house a den of thieves. He paid taxes—with money He got from a fish's mouth. And He spoke out openly against the hypocrisy of Jewish church leaders who used their power for their own good. Jesus did justly.

Jesus healed the sick, made the blind see, and enabled the lame to walk. He freed people from demons and illness. He reached out to Samaritans, prostitutes, and tax collectors, to sinners like you and me. Jesus loved mercy.

Jesus submitted to God's will to the point of dying on a cross. After His agonized prayers in Gethsemane, Jesus ultimately agreed to do the Father's will, not His own. Jesus walked humbly with His God. May we walk in our Savior's footprints.

100 Favorite Bible Verses

He has shown you, O man, what is good;
And what does the LORD require of you
But to do justly,
To love mercy,
And to walk humbly with your God?

MICAH 6:8

[Jesus] said, "Abba, Father, all things are possible for You. Take this cup away from Me; nevertheless, not what I will, but what You will."

MARK 14:36

Humble yourselves in the sight of the Lord, and He will lift you up.

JAMES 4:10

"Whoever desires to become great among you, let him be your servant. And whoever desires to be first among you, let him be your slave—just as the Son of Man did not come to be served, but to serve, and to give His life a ransom for many."

MATTHEW 20:26—28

WORSHIPING GOD

Praise and worship of God are always acts of will. Sometimes our problems or the burdens we carry choke out our good intentions, so we have to make the effort to establish praise as a way of life. And it becomes a way of life when we make it our first reaction to what we face and not a last resort. That's when we find true freedom in the Lord. . . .

In the Old Testament, the people who carried the Ark of the Covenant stopped every six steps to worship. We, too, need to remind ourselves not to go very far without stopping to worship. For spiritual well-being, we have to be six-step persons and continually invite the presence of the Lord to rule in our situations. We have to be free to praise Him no matter what our circumstances.

STORMIE OMARTIAN

Praying God's Will for Your Life

Give unto the LORD, O you mighty ones,
Give unto the LORD glory and strength.
Give unto the LORD the glory due to His name;
Worship the LORD in the beauty of holiness.

PSALM 29:1—2

Oh come, let us worship and bow down;
Let us kneel before the LORD our Maker.
For He is our God,
And we are the people of His pasture,
And the sheep of His hand.

PSALM 95:6—7

"The hour is coming, and now is, when the
true worshipers will worship the Father in
spirit and truth; for the Father is seeking such
to worship Him. God is Spirit, and those who
worship Him must worship in spirit and truth."

JOHN 4:23—24

JESUS IS ENOUGH

Jesus didn't live an easy life or die an easy death. The glory of Easter was preceded by the sorrow of absolute rejection. Our Redeemer knows what it feels like to be stripped of all comfort and ease. He experienced the betrayal of best friends. He sobbed alone, without a single person offering support. Yet, instead of trying to drown His sorrows with a margarita or spilling His guts to a sympathetic stranger on a plane, He endured. He shouldered the greatest possible anguish, being completely abandoned by everyone, including God, so we would never have to carry that burden ourselves.

I didn't used to believe Jesus was enough for me. . . . It wasn't until I hit the bottom that I found the love of Christ really is enough to sustain me, no matter what. Buckling under the weight of my own life is what helped me fall into the arms of God. I didn't just stumble into His grace; I collapsed there in a messy heap! And you know what? It's by far the best thing that's ever happened to me.

LISA HARPER

Stumbling into Grace

He is despised and rejected by men,
A Man of sorrows and acquainted with grief.
And we hid, as it were, our faces from Him;
He was despised, and we did not esteem Him.

ISAIAH 53:3

[Jesus] sat down with the twelve. Now as they
were eating, He said, "Assuredly, I say to you, one
of you will betray Me." . . . Jesus said to [Peter],
"Assuredly, I say to you that this night, before the
rooster crows, you will deny Me three times." . . .
[Jesus] began to be sorrowful and deeply
distressed. Then He said to [His disciples],
"My soul is exceedingly sorrowful, even to
death. Stay here and watch with Me." . . .
He came to the disciples and found them
sleeping, and said to Peter, "What! Could
you not watch with Me one hour?"

MATTHEW 26:20–21, 34, 37–38, 40

Against You, You only, have I sinned, . . .
Purge me with hyssop, and I shall be clean;
Wash me, and I shall be whiter than snow.

PSALM 51:4, 7

SCANDALOUS GRACE

May I just say something and get it out into the open? We're all dysfunctional.

There isn't one of us who hasn't "functioned abnormally" at some point in time. There isn't one of us who has skated through life without an impairment of some sort tagging behind her. . . .

Listen: I struggle. I dream. I aspire to be more like Jesus.

And on other days? Well, I think I'm as much like Him as I care to be.

Ah, such is the marvelous journey of life.

I am convinced that most women could stand a heaping dose of scandalous grace that enables them to cut themselves—as well as one another—some serious slack. . . . It is this grace . . . that truly becomes the icing on the cake of life—freeing us as women and provoking us to live outwardly with mercy and forgiveness toward one another and ourselves.

JULIE ANN BARNHILL

Scandalous Grace

Have mercy upon me, O God,
According to Your lovingkindness;
According to the multitude of
Your tender mercies,
Blot out my transgressions.
Wash me thoroughly from my iniquity,
And cleanse me from my sin.

PSALM 51:1—2

Since we are receiving a kingdom which
cannot be shaken, let us have grace,
by which we may serve God acceptably
with reverence and godly fear.

HEBREWS 12:28

[The Lord] said to me [Paul], "My grace is
sufficient for you, for My strength is made
perfect in weakness." Therefore most gladly
I will rather boast in my infirmities, that the
power of Christ may rest upon me. Therefore I
take pleasure in infirmities, in reproaches, in
needs, in persecutions, in distresses, for Christ's
sake. For when I am weak, then I am strong.

2 CORINTHIANS 12:9—10

NEW BEGINNINGS

Many situations in life—graduation, starting a new job, moving out on your own—are brand-new beginnings, a fresh start, a chance to try again or to try something completely new.

These aren't the only fresh starts you'll experience in life, however. God offers you a "beginning-again" ceremony every time you need a second chance. Whenever you blow it, make a poor choice, or even all-out rebel, God says, "Let's begin again." You don't have to go to a job interview or sign a new lease. All God asks is that you come to Him in honest repentance and ask His forgiveness. From that moment, the past truly is history. All is forgiven, and your fresh start is ready to commence.

Living God's Way

· · · · · · · · · ·

"I, even I, am He who blots out your
transgressions for My own sake;
And I will not remember your sins."

ISAIAH 43:25

If we confess our sins, He is faithful
and just to forgive us our sins and to
cleanse us from all unrighteousness.

1 JOHN 1:9

For as the heavens are high above the earth,
So great is His mercy toward those who fear Him;
As far as the east is from the west,
So far has He removed our
transgressions from us.

PSALM 103:11—12

TAKING A BREAK
FROM HEARTACHE

I have yet to meet a humorist, a comedian, or a clown who didn't have some deep hurt at the heart of his or her humor. When we laugh at something, we are in essence saying, "I identify with that!" If someone stood up and described all their blessings, we would be disgusted. When they stand up and share all their faults and foibles, we laugh and love them for it. Rosita Perez kindly encouraged me in a letter with these words: "Whoever says laughter isn't healing just hasn't hurt enough."

Laughter does not mean you are ignoring pain, living in denial, or just not aware of the troubles around you. . . . For me, laughter is how we take a much-needed break from the heartache, such that when we turn to face it again, it has by some miracle grown smaller in size and intensity, if not disappeared altogether.

LIZ CURTIS HIGGS

Only Angels Can Wing It

The LORD also will be a refuge for the oppressed,
A refuge in times of trouble.
And those who know Your name
will put their trust in You;
For You, LORD, have not forsaken
those who seek You.

PSALM 9:9–10

Weeping may endure for a night,
But joy comes in the morning.

PSALM 30:5

The fruit of the Spirit is love, joy, peace,
longsuffering, kindness, goodness,
faithfulness, gentleness, self-control.

GALATIANS 5:22–23

"I WILL NEVER
BE SHAKEN"

The Bible doesn't whitewash human nature or paint a picture of a pain-free world. Life is difficult, and the Bible doesn't suggest otherwise.

David was facing difficult times when he penned Psalm 62—"Truly he is my rock and my salvation; he is my fortress, I will never be shaken" (v. 2 NIV). Whatever the circumstances, David chose to focus on God. He reminded himself that God was his rock, a secure foundation for life.

Now consider the last part of this verse. Sounding entirely confident in his God, David proclaimed, "I will never be shaken." Nothing would rattle his faith! But the English Standard Version offers a glimpse of David's humanness: "I shall not be greatly shaken." This translation may be more real-life. Acknowledging at least implicitly the reality that events can shake—at least a little bit—the faith of even the most devoted follower, the psalmist vowed to "not be *greatly* shaken." The shaking doesn't last long. After all, the psalmist knows to turn to his Lord, who is his rock, his salvation, his fortress.

100 Favorite Bible Verses

"In the world you will have tribulation; but be
of good cheer, I have overcome the world."

JOHN 16:33

"I am with you always, even to the end of the age."

MATTHEW 28:20

The LORD is my rock and my
fortress and my deliverer;
My God, my strength, in whom I will trust;
My shield and the horn of my
salvation, my stronghold.

PSALM 18:2

GARDENING JOY

The garden looks as rumpled as clothes left in the dryer too long. It looks at you with the same accusing eyes. Enough beans remain for tonight's vegetable dish, but in this unpredicted heat wave isn't it easier to take something from the freezer? . . . Why bother? . . . Working in the garden offers an intimate contact with God through the earth and its power for growing things. . . .

If [you have] never known the thrill of growing things, try it! You have no need for a course in botany, biology, or chemistry. Just read the seed catalogues, the directions on the seed packets, start digging, raking, smoothing, and praying. There! Do you feel the surge of life beneath your hands? You are helping this earth (that God Himself planted in the beginning) to perpetuate life. Something happens between you and God that's very special and very intimate. Then, with the harvest, there comes a certain knowing that you have been in direct touch with the Creator. What joy!

JUNE MASTERS BACHER

Quiet Moments for Women

God blessed them, and God said to them. . . .
"See, I have given you every herb that
yields seed which is on the face of all the
earth, and every tree whose fruit yields
seed; to you it shall be for food."

GENESIS 1:28–29

The heavens declare the glory of God;
And the firmament shows His handiwork.

PSALM 19:1

Since the creation of the world [God's] invisible
attributes are clearly seen, being understood
by the things that are made, even His eternal
power and Godhead, so that [the unrighteous]
are without excuse [for not believing].

ROMANS 1:20

OUR EMPATHETIC
HERO

Mouthy, well-intentioned Peter, who'd vowed to stick to Jesus like Velcro, fell asleep while the Messiah mourned under those gnarled trees in the Garden of Gethsemane. Our Savior was bereft of companionship. No one dropped by with a pint of chicken soup. No one wrote Him a note expressing his or her condolences. Every single person abandoned Him during His time of deepest need. And that's why the author of Hebrews was able to preach, "God is the One who made all things, and all things are for his glory. He wanted to have many children share his glory, so he made the One who leads people to salvation perfect through suffering. . . . And now he can help those who are tempted, because he himself suffered and was tempted" (Hebrews 2:10, 18 NCV). Jesus didn't supernaturally skip to the front of the pain line. He chose instead to be an empathetic hero, sharing perfectly in the frailty and loneliness of our humanity.

LISA HARPER

Stumbling into Grace

Christ Jesus, who, being in the form of God, did not consider it robbery to be equal with God, but made Himself of no reputation, taking the form of a bondservant, and coming in the likeness of men. And being found in appearance as a man, He humbled Himself and became obedient to the point of death, even the death of the cross.

PHILIPPIANS 2:5–8

Christ also suffered once for sins, the just for the unjust, that He might bring us to God, being put to death in the flesh but made alive by the Spirit.

1 PETER 3:18

Surely He has borne our griefs
And carried our sorrows;
Yet we esteemed Him stricken,
Smitten by God, and afflicted.
But He was wounded for our transgressions,
He was bruised for our iniquities;
The chastisement for our peace was upon Him,
And by His stripes we are healed.

ISAIAH 53:4–5

RECAPTURING JOY

Is celebrating really that important anyway?

Yes, it is!

Life today is difficult. Problems challenge us, and we worry about our children's futures.

It's easy to fall into the trap of taking ourselves too seriously, of worrying about success, jobs, acceptance, parenting, illnesses, and so on. It's easy to lose our ability to laugh. It's easy to forget the simple ways of purely enjoying one another. Celebration keeps us balanced in a difficult world, renews our perspective, and enables us to recapture joy. It provides us with an easy means of building friendships within the family. A real benefit of celebration is that it can be very simple and yet the dividends are so great.

SUSAN ALEXANDER YATES

A House Full of Friends

Make a joyful shout to the LORD, all you lands!
Serve the LORD with gladness;
Come before His presence with singing.
Know that the LORD, He is God;
It is He who has made us, and not we ourselves;
We are His people and the sheep of His pasture.
Enter into His gates with thanksgiving,
And into His courts with praise.
Be thankful to Him, and bless His name.
For the LORD is good;
His mercy is everlasting,
And His truth endures to all generations.

PSALM 100:1—5

Rejoice always, pray without ceasing, in
everything give thanks; for this is the
will of God in Christ Jesus for you.

1 THESSALONIANS 5:16—18

A merry heart does good, like medicine.

PROVERBS 17:22

FEEDING YOUR SOUL

Think about that feeling of satisfaction you get when you've eaten a good meal of your favorite foods and you wisely choose to stop eating before you go from full to stuffed.

That's how God wants you to feel about life. A job well done, a dream fulfilled, a relationship healed, a confidence in knowing how much God loves you—there are numerous things God can bring your way that satisfy your heart.

God knows every one of your deepest desires. Trying to fill these desires on your own can lead to frustration—or even lead you away from God. But letting God fill your desires in His way and in His time leads to satisfaction that lasts.

Living God's Way

Delight yourself also in the LORD,
And He shall give you the desires of your heart.

PSALM 37:4

I will bless You while I live;
I will lift up my hands in Your name.
My soul shall be satisfied as with
marrow and fatness,
And my mouth shall praise You with joyful lips.

PSALM 63:4—5

Now to Him who is able to do exceedingly
abundantly above all that we ask or
think, according to the power that
works in us, to Him be glory.

EPHESIANS 3:20—21

SEEING GOD IN NATURE

Creation is a vivid expression of God's glory, power, and beauty. Those who recognize and appreciate the natural world as God's masterpiece are often quick to exclaim their admiration of it. How can we be silent in the presence of such magnificent beauty as a breathtaking sunset, a soaring mountain, or a raging river?

Indeed, natural beauty is one of the most unmistakable ways God reveals His character to us. Isn't the fact that He wants us to know Him enough to make you rejoice? The psalmist was rejoicing when he wrote the words, "I lift up my eyes to the hills. From where does my help come? My help comes from the LORD, who made heaven and earth" (Psalm 121:1–2).

When you look at creation, recognize God's greatness. The same God who created spectacular vistas and towering precipices is the God who comforts you in moments of weakness . . . who knew you before you were born . . . who offered His Son's life in exchange for yours. Consider His splendor, celebrate His glory, and rejoice!

A Jane Austen Devotional

For since the creation of the world His invisible attributes are clearly seen, being understood by the things that are made, even His eternal power and Godhead, so that they are without excuse.

ROMANS 1:20

"Where were you when I laid the
foundations of the earth?
Tell Me, if you have understanding.
Who determined its measurements?
Surely you know!
Or who stretched the line upon it?
To what were its foundations fastened?
Or who laid its cornerstone,
When the morning stars sang together,
And all the sons of God shouted for joy?"

JOB 38:4—7

The heavens declare the glory of God;
And the firmament shows His handiwork.

PSALM 19:1

A MATTER OF
THE HEART

C. S. Lewis once said, "No clever arrangement of bad eggs ever made a good omelet." What we truly are will dictate our choices, no matter how we try to camouflage or hide it, and no amount of moral effort will make us choose rightly if our hearts aren't right. . . .

Morality would be a cumbersome burden if each decision of our lives had to be carefully checked against some itemized, written code. We would be in constant turmoil worrying about whether some code was overlooked or misinterpreted. The joy of right living would be strangled in legalism. But it is exactly this sort of system that was in effect before Jesus brought the renovation of the human heart and motives through His death and resurrection and then provided us with the live-in support of the Holy Spirit. . . .

Good choices come most freely from the purist possible motives; these come from a heart repossessed by the transforming power of love. Love does what law could never do.

GLORIA GAITHER

Decisions

Owe no one anything except to love one another,
for he who loves another has fulfilled the
law. For the commandments, "You shall not
commit adultery," "You shall not murder,"
"You shall not steal," "You shall not bear
false witness," "You shall not covet," and if
there is any other commandment, are all
summed up in this saying, namely, "You
shall love your neighbor as yourself."

ROMANS 13:8–9

Sin shall not have dominion over you, for
you are not under law but under grace. What
then? Shall we sin because we are not under
law but under grace? Certainly not!

ROMANS 6:14–15

WHICH WAY
WAS I GOING?

When you were a kid, you may have dreamed about what you'd be when you grew up. At five, you pictured yourself as a superhero or a cowgirl. When you were fifteen, you might have imagined being a cheerleader or a drum major leading the band. Ultimately, you began a vocation after high school or college and thought you might have that job as a career for the rest of your life.

The problem is the rest of your life may change quickly. Devastating things happen in life and leave you feeling hopeless! You're suddenly set adrift, with nowhere to go and nowhere you want to go. You imagine the system has failed you or that God has left you.

Whatever the circumstances that bring a loss of your life direction, there is still reason to maintain a sense of hope. This kind of hope is built on trust in your Creator. He holds you up and has a plan for your life. He has your present and your future in His hands. Take comfort in that knowledge. He will plant new seeds of hope in your heart. Trust Him!

Little Seeds of Hope

Peace I leave with you, My peace I give to you;
not as the world gives do I give to you. Let not
your heart be troubled, neither let it be afraid.

JOHN 14:27

Are not two sparrows sold for a copper coin?
And not one of them falls to the ground apart
from your Father's will. But the very hairs of your
head are all numbered. Do not fear therefore;
you are of more value than many sparrows.

MATTHEW 10:29–31

We also glory in tribulations, knowing that
tribulation produces perseverance; and
perseverance, character; and character, hope.

ROMANS 5:3–4

PLANTING HOPE

Five years ago I planted over three hundred bulbs around a brick pathway and in varying places in our yard. I told my husband that I'd be able to manage the winter somehow if I could look forward to a spring and summertime filled with the vibrant colors of crocuses, daffodils, tulips, snowdrops, and lilies.

In a sense, I planted hope. The hope of new life. The products of sun and warmth.

When I feel my spirits drooping, I . . . envision all the lovely red, white, purple, pink, orange, and blue flowers that will explode in a wild proliferation of joy all over my yard, come spring.

When I can't find hope, hope has an exquisite way of finding me . . . through the promises of what will be.

JULIE ANN BARNHILL

Exquisite Hope

I will hope continually,
And will praise You yet more and more.

PSALM 71:14

Let love be without hypocrisy. . . . Be kindly
affectionate to one another with brotherly
love, in honor giving preference to one
another; . . . rejoicing in hope, patient in
tribulation, continuing steadfastly in prayer.

ROMANS 12:9–10, 12

Hope in the LORD;
For with the LORD there is mercy,
And with Him is abundant redemption.

PSALM 130:7

SINGLE AND CONTENT

Friends offer all sorts of advice to single women: don't be too aggressive or too backward, too friendly or too hard-to-get, too intellectual or too dumb, too earthly or too heavenly. "Hang around till the bitter end of the singles' barbecue—he might want to take you home." Or "Don't go to the singles' barbecue at all. Just stay home where you read your Bible and pray." It's terribly confusing.

"Is my Father God in charge here, or am I supposed to take over?" He is in charge if you want Him to be. He will not invade your freedom to choose to take over. But if you want His way—nothing more, nothing less, and nothing else—you've got to leave it to Him. It's easy to be deceived here telling ourselves we really want His will, but meaning "I want [God's will] so long as it includes marriage!"

God gives the very best to those who leave the choice with Him.

ELISABETH ELLIOT

Keep a Quiet Heart

· · · · · · ·

I know the plans I have for you, declares
the LORD, plans for welfare and not for
evil, to give you a future and a hope.

JEREMIAH 29:11 ESV

"Your kingdom come.
Your will be done
On earth as it is in heaven."

MATTHEW 6:10—22

Again, a second time, [Jesus] went
away and prayed, saying, "O My Father,
if this cup cannot pass away from Me
unless I drink it, Your will be done."

MATTHEW 26:42

Trust in the LORD with all your heart,
And lean not on your own understanding;
In all your ways acknowledge Him,
And He shall direct your paths.

PROVERBS 3:5—6

OUR THORNS,
GOD'S GRACE

No one knows what the thorn in Paul's flesh was (2 Corinthians 12:7). Whatever that affliction actually was does not matter. The truth God had taught Paul—and that Paul then taught us—matters greatly.

And what was that truth? That Jesus' grace was all he needed, whatever life's demands. Christ's power clearly rested on Paul in his weakness and enabled him to do what he wouldn't have been able to do on his own.

Paul had experienced God faithfully giving him strength when he was weak, insulted, persecuted, and struggling.

When we are aware of our weaknesses, of our need for Jesus, we yield ourselves more fully to God. We give Him room to move in and room to work. And He works not only in circumstances but also in our hearts. May we then, as Paul himself did, find delight in those weaknesses that help us know more fully God's great strength at work in us and through us.

100 Favorite Bible Verses

I can do all things through Christ
who strengthens me.

PHILIPPIANS 4:13

The LORD repay your work, and a full reward
be given you by the LORD God of Israel, under
whose wings you have come for refuge.

RUTH 2:12

To keep me grounded and stop me from
becoming too high and mighty due to the
extraordinary character of these revelations,
I was given a thorn in the flesh—a nagging
nuisance of Satan, a messenger to plague me!
I begged the Lord three times to liberate me
from its anguish; and finally He said to me, "My
grace is enough to cover and sustain you. My
power is made perfect in weakness." . . . I am at
peace and even take pleasure in any weaknesses,
insults, hardships, persecutions, and afflictions
for the sake of the Anointed because when I
am at my weakest, He makes me strong.

2 CORINTHIANS 12:7—10 THE VOICE

AUTHENTIC LOVE

A Zogby/Forbes ASAP poll asked respondents, *What would you like most to be known for? Being intelligent? Good looking? Having a great sense of humor?* A full half of respondents checked off an unexpected answer: They said they would like a reputation for "being authentic." In a world of spin and hype, the postmodern generation is searching desperately for something real and authentic. They will not take Christians seriously unless [we] demonstrate an authentic way of life. . . .

In the days of the early church, the thing that most impressed their neighbors in the Roman Empire was the community of love they witnessed among believers. "Behold how they love one another," it was said. In every age, the most persuasive evidence for the gospel is not words or arguments but a living demonstration of God's character through Christians' love for one another, expressed in both their words and their actions.

NANCY PEARCEY

Total Truth

Fulfill my joy by being like-minded, having the
same love, being of one accord, of one mind.

PHILIPPIANS 2:2

Love suffers long and is kind; love does not
envy; love does not parade itself, is not puffed
up; does not behave rudely, does not seek its
own, is not provoked, thinks no evil; does
not rejoice in iniquity, but rejoices in the
truth; bears all things, believes all things,
hopes all things, endures all things.

1 CORINTHIANS 13:4—7

All who believed were together, and had
all things in common, and sold their
possessions and goods, and divided
them among all, as anyone had need.
So continuing daily with one accord in the
temple, and breaking bread from house to
house, they ate their food with gladness and
simplicity of heart, praising God and having
favor with all the people. And the Lord added to
the church daily those who were being saved.

ACTS 2:44—47

BE A KID AGAIN

When Jesus said, "Let the little children come to me," He was talking to adults as well as kids. He was telling us to mimic the kids, to fling our hearts open wide and obliterate the boxes we've put God in. To embrace faith with wild abandon, be teachable, and trust God as a child would trust a parent. Sounds easy enough, right?

What can we learn from kids? To express our ideas boldly, to dream ginormous dreams, to live fully in the moment, to taste crazy foods, to take risks, to be wildly creative and contagiously optimistic, and to trust God wholeheartedly.

More Than a Bucket List

But Jesus said, "Let the little children
come to Me, and do not forbid them; for
of such is the kingdom of heaven."

MATTHEW 19:14

"Whoever comes to Me, and hears My sayings
and does them, I will show you whom he is
like: He is like a man building a house, who
dug deep and laid the foundation on the rock.
And when the flood arose, the stream beat
vehemently against that house, and could not
shake it, for it was founded on the rock."

LUKE 6:47–48

[Cast] all your care upon Him,
for He cares for you.

1 PETER 5:7

"PRAY WITHOUT CEASING"

Prayer is sort of like an unlocked door. . . . Inside is the storehouse of all that God is. He invites us to share it all. He doesn't intend for us to stay on the outside and struggle all alone with the perplexities of life, and He not only invites us to come in but to stay in, in order that His "grace and peace be yours in fullest measure, through the knowledge of God and Jesus our Lord" (2 Peter 1:2 NEB). . . .

It is an ongoing process, not just an occasional religious-sounding speech we make to a nebulous divinity "out there somewhere." Prayer is meant to be a part of our lives, like breathing and thinking and talking.

GLORIA GAITHER

Decisions

· · · · · · · · · ·

"I say to you, ask, and it will be given to you;
seek, and you will find; knock, and it will
be opened to you. For everyone who asks
receives, and he who seeks finds, and to him
who knocks it will be opened. If a son asks
for bread from any father among you, will he
give him a stone? Or if he asks for a fish, will
he give him a serpent instead of a fish?"

LUKE 11:9–11

Evening and morning and at noon
I will pray, and cry aloud,
And He shall hear my voice.

PSALM 55:17

Rejoice always, pray without ceasing, in
everything give thanks; for this is the
will of God in Christ Jesus for you.

1 THESSALONIANS 5:16–18

GOING HOME

Let's be honest. Old age entails suffering. I'm acutely aware of this now as I watch my mother, once so alive and alert and quick, now so quiet and confused and slow. She suffers. We who love her suffer. We see the "preview of coming attractions," ourselves in her shoes, and ponder what this interval means in terms of the glory of God in an old woman. . . .

We look at what's happening—limitations of hearing, seeing, moving, digesting, remembering; distortions of countenance, figure, and perspective. If that's all we could see, we'd certainly want a face-lift or something.

But we're on a pilgrim road. It's rough and steep, and it winds uphill to the very end. We can lift up our eyes and see the unseen: a Celestial City, a light, a welcome, an ineffable Face. We shall behold Him. We shall be like Him. And that makes a difference in how we go about aging.

ELISABETH ELLIOT

On Asking God Why

God will wipe away every tear from their eyes; there shall be no more death, nor sorrow, nor crying. There shall be no more pain, for the former things have passed away. Then He who sat on the throne said, "Behold, I make all things new."

REVELATION 21:4–5

Behold what manner of love the Father has bestowed on us, that we should be called children of God! Therefore the world does not know us, because it did not know Him. Beloved, now we are children of God; and it has not yet been revealed what we shall be, but we know that when He is revealed, we shall be like Him, for we shall see Him as He is.

1 JOHN 3:1–2

SOJOURNERS
ON EARTH

As believers, we understand the heart of the psalmist's declaration, "I am a sojourner on the earth" (Psalm 119:19 ESV); we simply aren't home yet. We are travelers, doing battle every day with failing bodies, corrupt political systems, poverty, squalor, chaos—all the deficiencies of living in a fallen world.

Do you ever feel an unexplainable homesickness? God designed us not to feel at peace in this world, but to always harbor homesickness. Our final resting place, heaven, will be the full manifestation of perfection. We will finally enjoy all that is missing here.

Though it's easy to get comfortable when our lives are going well, we should invite that longing. It is the living hope that something better awaits us. Remember, we're foreigners here. An existence not marred by imperfection or inadequacy is coming. A place that will know no more tears, no more sorrow. An eternity of communing freely with the God of the universe.

A Jane Austen Devotional

Now I saw a new heaven and a new earth, for the first heaven and the first earth had passed away. Also there was no more sea. Then I, John, saw the holy city, New Jerusalem, coming down out of heaven from God, prepared as a bride adorned for her husband. And I heard a loud voice from heaven saying, "Behold, the tabernacle of God is with men, and He will dwell with them, and they shall be His people. God Himself will be with them and be their God.

REVELATION 21:1–3

Our citizenship is in heaven, from which we also eagerly wait for the Savior, the Lord Jesus Christ.

PHILIPPIANS 3:20

"I, Jesus, have sent My angel to testify to you these things in the churches. I am the Root and the Offspring of David, the Bright and Morning Star." And the Spirit and the bride say, "Come!" And let him who hears say, "Come!" And let him who thirsts come. Whoever desires, let him take the water of life freely.

REVELATION 22:16–17

THE BIG PICTURE

The great evangelist Leonard Ravenhill was the last person on the planet you'd ever accuse of mincing words. "Five minutes after you die, you'll know how you should have lived."

You've got 1,440 minutes today; 43,200 this month; and 525,600 this year to determine your priorities and how you should be living. Even those minutes aren't guaranteed. So how will you live?

As distracted as we sometimes get, we can't afford to lose sight of the bigger picture—that heaven, our true home, awaits. Today carries real pain, struggle, and obligations, but never cast aside your "light and momentary troubles" for the eternal glory that outweighs them all (2 Corinthians 4:17)! Your citizenship in heaven begins on earth. Live a life that has heaven's flavor all over it.

More Than a Bucket List

Our citizenship is in heaven.

PHILIPPIANS 3:20

"Let not your heart be troubled; you believe
in God, believe also in Me. In My Father's
house are many mansions; if it were not so, I
would have told you. I go to prepare a place for
you. And if I go and prepare a place for you,
I will come again and receive you to Myself;
that where I am, there you may be also."

JOHN 14:1—3

Then He who sat on the throne said,
"Behold, I make all things new."

REVELATION 21:5

WHAT IF?

As an act of grace toward yourself, on this day imagine yourself to be the person you aspire to be. Spend the whole day walking in the blessing and persona of that person. What would you talk about? Where would you go? What kind of attitude would you have? How would you respond to the people around you? In what ways would your life look different?

What if you . . .

Dropped the spirit of criticism? Stopped blaming others? Were less defensive? Held your tongue this time? Jumped to a grace-filled conclusion instead? Had the courage to speak up for the underdog? Were brave enough to have that heart-stopping conversation?

Allow this one day to launch a lifetime of living as the person you aspire to be.

More Than a Bucket List

· · · · · · · · · ·

Be filled with the Spirit, speaking to one another
in psalms and hymns and spiritual songs,
singing and making melody in your heart to the
Lord, giving thanks always for all things to God
the Father in the name of our Lord Jesus Christ.

EPHESIANS 5:18—20

"The righteous will answer Him, saying, 'Lord,
when did we see You hungry and feed You, or
thirsty and give You drink? When did we see
You a stranger and take You in, or naked and
clothe You? Or when did we see You sick, or in
prison, and come to You?' And the King will
answer and say to them, 'Assuredly, I say to
you, inasmuch as you did it to one of the least
of these My brethren, you did it to Me.'"

MATTHEW 25:37—40

"You shall love your neighbor as yourself."

MATTHEW 19:19

A GRACIOUS HEART

No sooner had I turned forty, than I started receiving [e-mails] promoting products guaranteed to combat the effects of aging—they promise me younger, clearer skin; fewer wrinkles; no more dark shadows; more energy; prettier nails and hair; and improved eyesight and hearing. The implication is that, as I get older, what matters most is looking and feeling younger.

However, the fact is, I am getting older, and in this fallen world, that means my body is slowly deteriorating. I look in the mirror and see lines that weren't there ten years ago; I am definitely gray-headed. . . .

But I refuse to buy into the lie that those things are ultimate tragedies or that my biological clock can somehow be reversed. I am not trying to hasten my physical decline, but neither am I going to get consumed with fighting off the inevitable. As I get older, I want to focus on those things that God says matter most—things like letting His Spirit cultivate in me a gracious, wise, kind, loving heart.

NANCY LEIGH DEMOSS

Lies Women Believe

Our citizenship is in heaven, from which we also eagerly wait for the Savior, the Lord Jesus Christ, who will transform our lowly body that it may be conformed to His glorious body.

PHILIPPIANS 3:20—21

A gracious woman retains honor.

PROVERBS 11:16

As the elect of God, holy and beloved, put on tender mercies, kindness, humility, meekness, longsuffering.

COLOSSIANS 3:12

UNDESERVED!
Part 1

While many of us know Paul's explanation of salvation by heart—"For it is by grace you have been saved, through faith—and this is not from yourselves, it is the gift of God" (Ephesians 2:8 NIV)—most of us still water the plant of self-righteousness on the windowsill of our hearts. We may be thinking to ourselves that we're spiritually cleaner than the chick who smells like cigarette smoke in our Beth Moore Bible study. We may be assuming that our regular church attendance is adding up like divine frequent-flyer miles. Or we may secretly believe that we somehow *deserve* God's acceptance and approval more than the stinkers we rub shoulders with on a regular basis. . . .

I tend to see myself as more "forgiveness worthy" than people like my stepdad. I've made a habit of stroking and feeding an inner pet idol of *deservedness*. Sometimes I even buy little sweaters for it.

LISA HARPER

Stumbling into Grace

All have sinned and fall short of the glory of God.

ROMANS 3:23

Remember, O LORD, Your tender mercies
and Your lovingkindnesses,
For they are from of old.
Do not remember the sins of my
youth, nor my transgressions;
According to Your mercy remember me,
For Your goodness' sake, O LORD.

PSALM 25:6—7

"The Pharisee stood and prayed thus with
himself, 'God, I thank You that I am not like
other men—extortioners, unjust, adulterers,
or even as this tax collector.' . . . The tax
collector, standing afar off, would not so much
as raise his eyes to heaven, but beat his breast,
saying, 'God, be merciful to me a sinner!'
I tell you, this man went down to his house
justified rather than the other; for everyone
who exalts himself will be humbled, and he
who humbles himself will be exalted."

LUKE 18:11, 13—14

UNDESERVED!
Part 2

One of my dear friends had a daddy who was so mean she actually prayed for God to go ahead and take him out, if He wasn't planning on saving him. Of course, she was wholly undone when her father walked an aisle and gave his crooked heart to Jesus at the age of eighty-four! People. Messy people. Mistake-prone people. Even mean, old daddies. God loves them all. It is His will that none of us should perish. And He goes to extravagant lengths to accomplish His will.

May I [offer] a suggestion from one stinker to another? Make a short list of the people in your life story who appear to be the least deserving of God's forgiveness. Pray for them by name—that they will stumble into the redemptive grace of Jesus Christ—at least once a week. And for goodness' sake, instead of praying for God to take them out if He's not going to save them, ask Him to kill the idol of deservedness in your own heart!

LISA HARPER

Stumbling into Grace

The Lord is not slack concerning His
promise [to return], as some count
slackness, but is longsuffering toward
us, not willing that any should perish but
that all should come to repentance.

2 PETER 3:9

If you confess with your mouth the Lord Jesus
and believe in your heart that God has raised
Him from the dead, you will be saved.

ROMANS 10:9

"Look to Me, and be saved,
All you ends of the earth!
For I am God, and there is no other."

ISAIAH 45:22

DON'T MISS THE VIEW

"Let's pause a minute and enjoy the view," the guide said as the hikers stopped for breath on a nature walk at the Grand Canyon.

Everyone gasped in awe at the splendor spread below. The *huff-puff* of the steep mountain trail robbed the procession of a chance to see the cathedral-like monuments . . . time had carved along the way.

"Were those formations there when we passed?" one of the tourists teased.

The guide nodded seriously. "They were. But in our struggle to reach the top, we missed the view."

Guilty as charged. . . . Are we in such a rush to climb the ladder of success that we never look over our shoulders? So we reach the top . . . so we bump our heads on the very ceiling of achievement? How sad to realize one day that the rush to a destination robbed us of the joy of traveling.

JUNE MASTERS BACHER

The Quiet Heart

·······•••

[Jesus] said to [the apostles], "Come aside by
yourselves to a deserted place and rest a while."
For there were many coming and going, and they
did not even have time to eat. So they departed
to a deserted place in the boat by themselves.

MARK 6:31–32

Be still, and know that I am God.

PSALM 46:10

The LORD is my shepherd;
I shall not want.
He makes me to lie down in green pastures;
He leads me beside the still waters.
He restores my soul.

PSALM 23:1–3

GOD WILL NOT
LET US GO

Do you sometimes have a hard time finishing a project you start? Fortunately, our heavenly Father is not like that at all.

When God enables us to recognize our sin and our need for forgiveness, He won't stop until He finishes. And He won't consider Himself finished until the final product meets His high standards of purity, holiness, and—in eternity—Christlikeness. Furthermore, God is not surprised by the challenges that come with our lack of cooperation or the roadblocks we erect with our sinful ways and selfish desires. He expects hardened hearts and too-busy schedules. He knows we'll make wrong choices and have wrong priorities. Yet God will not let us go.

The Master Artist's signature reads *Yahweh*, and it's written on your heart, just as your name is written on the palms of His Son's hands. And the Artist who began that good work in you will indeed see it through to completion.

100 Favorite Bible Verses

I am persuaded that neither death nor life,
nor angels nor principalities nor powers,
nor things present nor things to come, nor
height nor depth, nor any other created thing,
shall be able to separate us from the love of
God which is in Christ Jesus our Lord.

ROMANS 8:38–39

Have you not known?
Have you not heard?
The everlasting God, the LORD,
The Creator of the ends of the earth,
Neither faints nor is weary.
His understanding is unsearchable.
He gives power to the weak,
And to those who have no might
He increases strength.

ISAIAH 40:28–29

Being confident of this very thing, that
He who has begun a good work in you will
complete it until the day of Jesus Christ.

PHILIPPIANS 1:6

MAKING A DIFFERENCE

You are a walking, talking message of hope. Whether you realize it or not, your character, words, and actions are all preaching a sermon to those you meet along the road of life. The closer you follow God, the more visible He'll be to others through you.

You may never know how wide your influence really goes. An act of kindness, a word of encouragement, or a job well done could be what moves a close friend, or even a stranger, one step closer to knowing God.

Take a moment to thank God for the people who've had a positive influence on your life. Then ask God to help you become someone else's reason for thanks.

Living God's Way

Do all things without complaining and disputing, that you may become blameless and harmless, children of God without fault in the midst of a crooked and perverse generation, among whom you shine as lights in the world.

PHILIPPIANS 2:14—15

Let nothing be done through selfish ambition or conceit, but in lowliness of mind let each esteem others better than himself. Let each of you look out not only for his own interests, but also for the interests of others.

PHILIPPIANS 2:3—4

"Let your light so shine before men, that they may see your good works and glorify your Father in heaven."

MATTHEW 5:16

ACCEPTING WHAT GOD GIVES

For my birthday one year, my mother sent me a package. . . . When I opened it, there was a gaudy, multicolored Mexican straw basket inside, stuffed with tissue paper. . . . I tossed out the tissue paper, wondered what in the world I was going to do with the basket, then called to thank her for her "gift." Mother laughed when I thanked her for the basket [and] then asked what I thought about what was inside it. I told her that nothing was inside except tissue paper, and I had thrown that out. . . .

"Oh no, Anne! Inside that tissue paper is your real birthday gift!"

I ran outside . . . and went through the garbage piece by piece until I came up with the wad of tissue paper. Inside was a small gold ring with a lapis lazuli stone. . . .

Sometimes God wraps His glory in hard circumstances or ugly obstacles or painful difficulties, and it just never occurs to us that within those life-shaking events is a fresh revelation of Him.

ANNE GRAHAM LOTZ

I Saw the Lord

"When you pass through the
waters, I will be with you;
And through the rivers, they
shall not overflow you.
When you walk through the fire,
you shall not be burned,
Nor shall the flame scorch you.
For I am the LORD your God."

ISAIAH 43:2

Every good gift and every perfect gift
is from above, and comes down from
the Father of lights, with whom there is
no variation or shadow of turning.

JAMES 1:17

"Do not judge according to appearance."

JOHN 7:24

HEALING YOUR HEART

Whatever you put your heart into usually gives you hope and joy. Your heart glows with love and gives you a reason to wake up each morning. You know there's a risk, but you take it because when it works well, it's the best gift ever. How can God understand this? He understands because He took the greatest risk of all. He loved us first before we ever loved Him. He set the wheels of love in motion.

When your heart is broken, certainly you know that God grieves with you. He recognizes the hope and the love you put into your relationship and that you need His comfort. Rest! Give Him a chance to draw near to you and give you His peace in your current situation. He is the One who can mend broken hearts and bring you new joy.

Your Promises from God Today

For God so loved the world that He gave His only begotten Son, that whoever believes in Him should not perish but have everlasting life.

JOHN 3:16

Draw near to God and He will draw near to you. Cleanse your hands, you sinners; and purify your hearts, you double-minded.

JAMES 4:8

Therefore know that the LORD your God, He is God, the faithful God who keeps covenant and mercy for a thousand generations with those who love Him and keep His commandments.

DEUTERONOMY 7:9

SEEING POTENTIAL

Secondhand shopping hones your ability to see something that others may not—potential. The ability to see something not for what it is but instead for what it can be is a great gift. If I . . . bought the five-piece furniture set with matching lamps for each room in my house, it wouldn't really be worth mentioning. . . . If I piece together hand-me-downs and create a beautiful space, well, that's something special. I want to challenge you to start looking at things—and people and situations—for what they can be, not what they are. I think you'll find treasures in all aspects of your life, treasures that have been hiding right under your nose. . . .

I've always loved the fact that God sees potential in each of us, no matter how big we've messed up or how broken we are. Isn't it awesome that we can take that example and do the same thing—not only in castoff furniture, but in others and even in ourselves? I'm incredibly thankful for potential. It means that in the right hands, the ordinary can become extraordinary.

MARIAN PARSONS

Inspired You

The LORD said to Samuel, "Do not look at his appearance or at his physical stature, because I have refused him. For the LORD does not see as man sees; for man looks at the outward appearance, but the LORD looks at the heart."

1 SAMUEL 16:7

Blessed is the Lord God of Israel,
For He has visited and redeemed His people.

LUKE 1:68

I know that my Redeemer lives,
And He shall stand at last on the earth;
And after my skin is destroyed, this I know,
That in my flesh I shall see God.

JOB 19:25—26

SILVER LINING

No doubt Noah felt the grace (unmerited favor) of God when he was delivered from the total destruction that wiped out sinful humankind. For Noah, God brought forth treasure in the darkness when the flood ended. Noah again heard the voice of God and beheld the bow in the clouds. Here was the assurance of God's presence and comfort, along with His faithfulness and ongoing promise.

Those same treasures are there for each of us as we come through crisis or struggle, for as we look for the silver lining in each cloud, we discover the treasure He has hidden there. All is not lost, and He is forever with us to comfort and encourage us no matter what happens on this earth. If we find our feet stuck in the cloud of passing crisis, perhaps it's God's way of asking us to go back and check for the silver lining!

LANA BATEMAN

Women of Faith Devotional Bible

It shall be, when I bring a cloud over the
earth, that the rainbow shall be seen in the
cloud; and I will remember My covenant
which is between Me and you and every living
creature of all flesh; the waters shall never
again become a flood to destroy all flesh.

GENESIS 9:14–15

Be strong and of good courage, do not fear
nor be afraid of them; for the LORD your
God, He is the One who goes with you.
He will not leave you nor forsake you.

DEUTERONOMY 31:6

David said to his son Solomon, "Be strong and
of good courage, and do it; do not fear nor be
dismayed, for the LORD God—my God—will
be with you. He will not leave you nor forsake
you, until you have finished all the work
for the service of the house of the LORD."

1 CHRONICLES 28:20

A PICTURE OF FAITH

Look out several feet past the shore and you may see a group of people, even children, standing in what appears to be just a few feet of water. How is that possible, when you see others closer in, swimming in water that's over their heads?

Sandbars are formed at the break point of waves, and not all of them are visible. It's great fun to discover one beneath the ocean's surface. . . .

Our faith can be a lot like finding that "hidden" sandbar: we are willing to take that deep step, because we're certain it's out there—somewhere.

Understandably, sandbars are also navigational nightmares to boats and can cause considerable damage. . . .

From a faith perspective, it's an interesting visual. On one side of the sandbar, some are eager to swim toward it, unconcerned about the depth of the waters surrounding it. On the other side, others want nothing to do with it, and they change course at any hint of its presence. . . .

On which side of the sandbar does your faith reside?

MIRIAM DRENNAN

Devotions for the Beach

Now faith is the substance of things hoped
for, the evidence of things not seen.

HEBREWS 11:1

In You, O LORD, I put my trust;
Let me never be ashamed;
Deliver me in Your righteousness.
Bow down Your ear to me,
Deliver me speedily;
Be my rock of refuge,
A fortress of defense to save me.
For You are my rock and my fortress;
Therefore, for Your name's sake,
Lead me and guide me.

PSALM 31:1—3

Moses called Joshua and said to him in the sight
of all Israel, "Be strong and of good courage. . . .
And the LORD, He is the One who goes before
you. He will be with you, He will not leave you
nor forsake you; do not fear nor be dismayed."

DEUTERONOMY 31:7—8

PRESENT SUFFERINGS,
FUTURE GLORY

The apostle Paul dearly loved the elders of the Ephesian church, and when he visited them on his way to Jerusalem, he wasn't sure if he would ever see them again this side of heaven. Paul acknowledged the risks inherent in his trip: "chains and tribulations await me" (Acts 20:23).

Then came Paul's bold proclamation in verse 24: those dangers and risks were not going to keep him from going to Jerusalem. What mattered most to Paul was not how long his life lasted, but that—however many days God gave him—he would "finish [his] race with joy."

Paul was confident that the Lord had called him "to testify to the gospel of the grace of God," and he had faithfully fulfilled that calling, often at great cost to his physical health and safety. And he was willing to suffer some more.

What an example for us! May we, like Paul, finish our earthly race with joy!

100 Favorite Bible Verses

I consider that the sufferings of this present time are not worthy to be compared with the glory which shall be revealed in us. For the earnest expectation of the creation eagerly waits for the revealing of the sons of God.

ROMANS 8:18—19

We do not lose heart. Even though our outward man is perishing, yet the inward man is being renewed day by day. For our light affliction, which is but for a moment, is working for us a far more exceeding and eternal weight of glory, while we do not look at the things which are seen, but at the things which are not seen. For the things which are seen are temporary, but the things which are not seen are eternal.

2 CORINTHIANS 4:16—18

We also glory in tribulations, knowing that tribulation produces perseverance; and perseverance, character; and character, hope.

ROMANS 5:3—4

ACROSS THE MILES

Events like graduation day, a big move, or a new job can bring excitement, change, expectation—and good-byes. A lot of the people you've grown close to over the past several years may not be headed the same direction that God is leading you. But that doesn't mean your friendships can't continue to grow.

Keeping in touch across the miles takes effort. However, an email, a crazy card, or a heartfelt phone call is all a friendship needs to spark many happy reunions. The friends God brings into your life are worth holding onto and praying for. That includes the ones you haven't met yet.

Along with those good-byes, you're also going to be saying a lot of glad-to-meet-yous. So open your heart. Some of your very best friends are waiting to meet you.

Living God's Way

· · · · · · · · ·

"Greater love has no one than this, than
to lay down one's life for his friends."

JOHN 15:13

A friend loves at all times.

PROVERBS 17:17

Iron sharpens iron,
and one man sharpens another.

PROVERBS 27:17 ESV

The righteous should choose
his friends carefully.

PROVERBS 12:26

WHAT LOVE LOOKS LIKE

Want to know what love looks like? Look at God. Consider His sacrifice, His patience, His comfort, His faithfulness, His generosity. God's creativity in expressing love is so great that it's almost incomprehensible.

Consider how your love stands up next to His. Don't get discouraged. You're not God. At times, your love still falters and fails—but God's love is always at work in your life. He's helping you love others in the same wonderful way He so deeply loves you.

Let God's creative compassion inspire you to love others well. Ask for His help in knowing the best way to express your love so that it meets needs, builds relationships, and warms hearts. Then take a moment to sit back and enjoy His love for you.

Living God's Way

. . . .

Above all things have fervent love for one
another, for "love will cover a multitude of sins."

1 PETER 4:8

"God so loved the world that He gave His only
begotten Son, that whoever believes in Him
should not perish but have everlasting life."

JOHN 3:16

Love suffers long and is kind; love does not
envy; love does not parade itself, is not puffed
up; does not behave rudely, does not seek its
own, is not provoked, thinks no evil; does not
rejoice in iniquity, but rejoices in the truth;
bears all things, believes all things, hopes all
things, endures all things. Love never fails.

1 CORINTHIANS 13:4–8

EMBRACE TRUTH AND
FIND GOD'S GRACE

I know what it's like to have a past you'd just as soon forget. A past that you had no control over—your family of origin; your mother's choice of lifestyle; your family's battle with alcohol—as well as a past of misgivings made by your own free will. . . .

We all have "issues." We all carry burdens and regrets. And we all play a shell game of sorts, hoping to hide and deflect the broken places of our lives. But I say it's time to embrace truth.

So why not:

- Embrace the fact that you are a mess of magnificent proportions?
- Embrace the fact that you are not alone?
- Embrace the lavish reality of divine grace . . . that heals, restores, covers, forgives, renews, and abounds?

What true freedom!

JULIE ANN BARNHILL

Scandalous Grace

If we confess our sins, He is faithful
and just to forgive us our sins and to
cleanse us from all unrighteousness.

1 JOHN 1:9

The LORD is my shepherd;
I shall not want.
He makes me to lie down in green pastures;
He leads me beside the still waters.
He restores my soul.

PSALM 23:1–3

Have mercy upon me, O God,
According to Your lovingkindness;
According to the multitude
of Your tender mercies,
Blot out my transgressions.
Wash me thoroughly from my iniquity,
And cleanse me from my sin.
For I acknowledge my transgressions. . . .
Wash me, and I shall be whiter than snow.

PSALM 51:1–3, 7

INDEPENDENCE DAY

Life is full of starting-over days, days that often feel like a fresh taste of freedom. The choices and changes that are right around the corner seem sweet and exciting because the direction you choose to go is now solely up to you—and God.

Being dependent on God doesn't interfere with that newfound freedom. Relying on God for guidance, strength, comfort, wisdom, and countless other gifts allows you to risk throwing yourself wholeheartedly into the adventure of life. It's like having a partner belay your rope while rock climbing. It gives you the freedom and courage to tackle higher and harder climbs. The closer the partnership you have with God, the freer you'll find you are to reach your true potential.

Living God's Way

"Fear not, for I am with you;
Be not dismayed, for I am your God.
I will strengthen you,
Yes, I will help you,
I will uphold you with My righteous right hand."

ISAIAH 41:10

Trust in the LORD with all your heart,
And lean not on your own understanding;
In all your ways acknowledge Him,
And He shall direct your paths.

PROVERBS 3:5—6

Even the youths shall faint and be weary,
And the young men shall utterly fall,
But those who wait on the LORD
Shall renew their strength;
They shall mount up with wings like eagles,
They shall run and not be weary,
They shall walk and not faint.

ISAIAH 40:30—31

LEARNING TO REST

I'm so glad Jesus advocated rest for His follow-ers. He doesn't guilt us into overdoing it even when it comes to ministry. Instead He teaches us (and modeled for us according to Mark 1:35 and Luke 4:42) to slow down and recuperate after giving our all for the sake of the gospel. To find a balance between *going out and doing* and *being still and knowing*. Resting—learning to weave practical Sabbaths into our schedules—isn't a punitive decree; it's God's generous endow-ment for our protection and perseverance. And I think Matthew narrated Jesus' words regard-ing this gift better than anyone else:

> Are you tired? Worn out? Burned out on religion? Come to me. Get away with me and you'll recover your life. I'll show you how to take a real rest. Walk with me and work with me—watch how I do it. Learn the unforced rhythms of grace. I won't lay anything heavy or ill-fitting on you. Keep company with me and you'll learn to live freely and lightly. (Matthew 11:28–30 MSG)

LISA HARPER

Stumbling into Grace

In the morning, having risen a long while
before daylight, [Jesus] went out and departed
to a solitary place; and there He prayed.

MARK 1:35

When it was day, [Jesus] departed
and went into a deserted place.

LUKE 4:42

"You shall keep the Sabbath, therefore,
for it is holy to you. . . . Work shall be
done for six days, but the seventh is the
Sabbath of rest, holy to the LORD."

EXODUS 31:14—15

BE A HERO

Heroism is not always about rushing into a burning building. Look around. Heroic moments are happening everywhere. Whether it's helping an elderly person pump gas, checking up on a neighbor, or helping an overtaxed waitress remember her order, you can be someone's hero. Anytime. Anywhere.

To be others-focused means to be conscious of the conversation in your head and to flip the switch from "me" and "mine" to "us" and "ours." Think in terms of generosity, sacrifice, connection, noticing, and giving.

More Than a Bucket List

Do nothing from selfishness or empty conceit, but with humility of mind regard one another as more important than yourselves; do not merely look out for your own personal interests, but also for the interests of others.

PHILIPPIANS 2:3—4 NASB

"Whoever desires to become great among you shall be your servant. And whoever of you desires to be first shall be slave of all. For even the Son of Man did not come to be served, but to serve, and to give His life a ransom for many."

MARK 10:43—45

Yet who knows whether you have come to the kingdom for such a time as this?

ESTHER 4:14

LINGER WITH
YOUR LORD

There are days we race through, as though God is an item to check off our "to do" lists. . . . Then there are times when those clamoring voices vying for attention will just have to wait; you want to spend time with your Maker. . . . You want nothing more than to be still in Him. So you linger, remaining there as long as possible because of the peace, the comfort, and the rest you feel. . . .

When you experience those moments, drink deeply. Receive Jesus, welcome Him, linger with Him. As in any good conversation, give Him time to speak and yourself time to listen. If your soul feels parched, ask Him to quench it in this way. When the day becomes busy, as it surely will, stay mindful that He remains with you. He is there and present.

This was Jesus' promise to the disciples and to us as He returned to the Father. We may not completely understand how He does this, but we can be certain that this is no hurdle for the One who conquered death.

MIRIAM DRENNAN

Devotions for the Beach

"Surely I am with you always, to
the very end of the age."
MATTHEW 28:20 NIV

"Come to Me, all you who labor and are
heavy laden, and I will give you rest."
MATTHEW 11:28

[Jesus] said to them, "Come aside by yourselves
to a deserted place and rest a while."
MARK 6:31

MOST IMPORTANT

Isn't it so easy to get preoccupied with our homes (and our lives) needing to be perfect or at least appearing that way? . . . This pursuit of impossible perfection can easily overshadow the things in life that should be more important, like our families and our faith. I have to remind myself (on many occasions) that there are more valuable pursuits than clutter-free counters, perfectly fluffed pillows, and spot-free slipcovers. It doesn't mean those things are wrong, but when that is the focus of my daily life, I've got a problem.

When we're striving for domestic perfection, we're missing the mark. If our highest priority is walking in faith and loving our families, we'll find joy in the sofa stains, the scratches on the dining room table, and the pile of shoes by the door. We'll be able to show love and grace when a child draws on the wall with a crayon or a husband leaves tools all over the counter. Most important, we will let the people in our lives know that we love them and that their mess doesn't take away from that.

MARIAN PARSONS

Inspired You

· · · · · · · · · ·

"Seek first the kingdom of God
and His righteousness."

MATTHEW 6:33

"Teacher, which is the great
commandment in the law?"
Jesus said to him, "'You shall love the
LORD your God with all your heart, with
all your soul, and with all your mind.'
This is the first and great commandment.
And the second is like it: 'You shall
love your neighbor as yourself.'"

MATTHEW 22:36—39

When [Jesus] had called the people to
Himself, with His disciples also, He said to
them, "Whoever desires to come after Me,
let him deny himself, and take up his cross,
and follow Me. For whoever desires to save
his life will lose it, but whoever loses his
life for My sake and the gospel's will save it.
For what will it profit a man if he gains the
whole world, and loses his own soul?"

MARK 8:34—36

WHAT A PRIVILEGE!

Wisdom, power, and wealth—God warns us against pridefully finding glory in these. In Jeremiah 9:23–24, God calls us to glory in the fact that we know and understand Him. That is a rather mind-boggling reality—you have been invited to know and to be in relationship with the Creator, Sustainer, and sovereign Ruler of the universe. Knowing Him means seeing Him when others don't. You see His loving-kindness in the way He faithfully answers your prayers and provides for all your needs. You find hope and peace in the truth that He will one day exercise judgment against the immoral and ungodly. You see His righteousness in His commands, and you look forward to the ultimate victory when Jesus returns to reign in righteousness.

What a privilege to know the Lord! May your time spent reading God's Word, worshiping the Lord, and praying to Him bring you great joy day in and day out. Glory in the fact that you know the Lord!

100 Favorite Bible Verses

"Let not the wise man glory in his wisdom,
Let not the mighty man glory in his might,
Nor let the rich man glory in his riches;
But let him who glories glory in this,
That he understands and knows Me,
That I am the LORD, exercising lovingkindness,
judgment, and righteousness in the earth.
For in these I delight," says the LORD.

JEREMIAH 9:23–24

All that is in the world—the lust of the flesh,
the lust of the eyes, and the pride of life—is
not of the Father but is of the world.

1 JOHN 2:16

Humble yourselves in the sight of the
Lord, and He will lift you up.

JAMES 4:10

LOVE AND MARRIAGE

Marriage is not something that can be improvised. You are both embarking on a long voyage, untrained, in a frail little boat headed, inevitably, for stormy waters. . . . There may be some days when you are safely anchored in the harbor, but that's not what boats are built for. They are built for sea travel.

Walter and I had a few safe harbor days, but most of the time it seemed we were out on the ocean, bailing water, pulling people from the ocean and into the boat, and trying to keep our own signals straight as husband and wife. During those times we needed our strong copilot, the Holy Spirit of God. And we needed the encouragement of fellow Christians who would cheer us on from their own boats nearby. . . .

Love is a decision, a judgment. It involves the intellect and the will. . . . I am reminded of a statement by Dr. Bovet: "First you choose the one you love and then you love the one you have chosen."

INGRID TROBISCH

The Hidden Strength

A threefold cord is not quickly broken.

ECCLESIASTES 4:12

"'A man shall leave his father and mother
and be joined to his wife, and the two
shall become one flesh'; so then they
are no longer two, but one flesh."

MARK 10:7–8

Be filled with the Spirit . . . giving thanks
always for all things to God the Father in the
name of our Lord Jesus Christ, submitting
to one another in the fear of God. Wives,
submit to your own husbands, as to the Lord.
For the husband is head of the wife, as also
Christ is head of the church . . . Husbands,
love your wives, just as Christ also loved
the church and gave Himself for her.

EPHESIANS 5:18, 20-22, 25

YOUR SHEPHERD'S VOICE

The Eastern shepherd of Jesus' day raised his sheep primarily in the Judean uplands. The countryside was rocky, hilly, and filled with deep crevices and ravines. Patches of grass were sparse. So the shepherd had to establish a personal, working relationship with each sheep, developing its love and trust in him in order to lead it to where the path was the smoothest, the pasture was the greenest, the water was the cleanest, and the nights were the safest. The shepherd always *led* the sheep. He knew their names, and when he called them, they recognized his voice, following him like a swarm of little chicks follows the mother hen. When he stopped, the sheep huddled closely around him, pressing against his legs. Their personal relationship with him was based on his voice, which they knew and trusted.

Our Good Shepherd is Jesus, and the voice of the Good Shepherd is the Word of God. Our Shepherd speaks to us through the written words of our Bible, and His words are personal.

ANNE GRAHAM LOTZ

I Saw the Lord

"I am the good shepherd; and I know My sheep, and am known by My own. As the Father knows Me, even so I know the Father; and I lay down My life for the sheep."

JOHN 10:14—15

"The sheep hear [the shepherd's] voice; and he calls his own sheep by name and leads them out. And when he brings out his own sheep, he goes before them; and the sheep follow him, for they know his voice."

JOHN 10:3—4

I will delight myself in Your commandments, Which I love.

PSALM 119:47

BLESSED TO BE
A BLESSING

My grandmother never went out and purchased a new hat to combat the blahs. Money didn't grow on sassafras bushes; and, besides, she preferred a sunbonnet. But, oh yes, she had a cure. "Let's do something impulsive!" she used to say. "Let's go for a tramp in the woods. . . ."

When we'd come home we'd do an impulsive deed for a neighbor. Today, I looked back and tried to recall some of the things we did—because they're exactly what I plan to do!

- Write a letter when it's not your turn!
- Call somebody you haven't heard from in years;
- Make a batch of cookies and take them to a shut-in; and
- Go out and look for a stranger to smile at!

JUNE MASTERS BACHER

Quiet Moments for Women

Remember the words of the Lord Jesus, that He said, "It is more blessed to give than to receive."

ACTS 20:35

Our mouth was filled with laughter,
And our tongue with singing.
Then they said among the nations,
"The LORD has done great things for them."

PSALM 126:2

I will bless you. . . .
And you shall be a blessing.

GENESIS 12:2

YOUR WONDERFUL
UNIQUENESS

When I was growing up and obsessing about the size of my nose (substantial), my grandmother used to tell me, "It gives you character." I distinctly recall thinking that I could've done with a little less "character." She would also remind me in my insecure moments that people were not thinking about me as much as I imagined they were. She said that they were all doing the same thing I was doing: wondering what others were thinking of *them*. If I could reclaim a chunk of lost time and wasted emotional energy, I would wish to have back all the moments I spent lost in those useless thoughts.

If beauty is in the eye of the beholder, your wonderful uniqueness is precisely what brings God pleasure. It gives you "character," and He's smitten with you. So don't just embrace your uniqueness; revel in it.

ANITA RENFROE

The Purse-Driven Life

Your hands have made me and fashioned me;
Give me understanding,
that I may learn Your commandments.

PSALM 119:73

God has dealt to each one a measure of faith.
For as we have many members in one body, but
all the members do not have the same function,
so we, being many, are one body in Christ,
and individually members of one another.
Having then gifts differing according to the
grace that is given to us, let us use them.

ROMANS 12:3–6

You are He who took Me out of the womb;
You made Me trust while on My mother's breasts.
I was cast upon You from birth.
From My mother's womb
You have been My God.

PSALM 22:9–10

TRANSFORMATION

Have you ever considered the humble beginnings of sea glass? All of it starts as glass that has been thrown away, discarded, and broken. Pieces of a former whole no longer serve their intended purpose, so they are cast away—then tossed about, taking some hard knocks, and finally emerging smooth, refined, beautiful.

Likewise, there are those days, even seasons, when we feel fragmented and useless. . . . Parts of a former whole, we find ourselves being tossed about, taking hard knocks, unsure of our direction or purpose.

The Father knows, and sometimes orchestrates, our seasons of refinement—it is part of a greater plan, His plan, which serves His purposes. Even when we're on the other side of that season, we may still not understand fully the *why* behind it, but we can be sure we have a Father who loves us, pursues us, and—once His hand is upon us—does not let go.

Trust that during these seasons, we are being refined and transformed into something useful. And ultimately, beautiful.

MIRIAM DRENNAN

Devotions for the Beach

You, O God, have tested us;
You have refined us as silver is refined.

PSALM 66:10

For I know the plans I have for you, declares
the LORD, plans for welfare and not for
evil, to give you a future and a hope.

JEREMIAH 29:11 ESV

"My sheep hear My voice, and I know them, and
they follow Me. And I give them eternal life, and
they shall never perish; neither shall anyone
snatch them out of My hand. My Father, who has
given them to Me, is greater than all; and no one
is able to snatch them out of My Father's hand."

JOHN 10:27—29

THE RIGHT GOAL

Goals are a good thing. Focus in a particular direction helps you move forward. When you feel stuck or you're not quite reaching the goal you intended, it can present an opportunity. It can give you a chance to look at your goals and see if you're going after the right ones, the goals God designed for your life. You may be surprised. If your goal is truly the one God wants for you, then go for it. Be in it to win it! If your goal is not really part of His plan for you, then step back and take another look.

It always helps to seek the counsel of others when you're going after a goal. Who do you know right now who could mentor you or give you some wise advice? Pray, seek God's advice, and then head out with confidence to do the things you are truly meant to do today.

Your Promises from God Today

· · · · · · · · · · ·

I can of Myself do nothing. As I hear, I judge; and My judgment is righteous, because I do not seek My own will but the will of the Father who sent Me.

JOHN 5:30

Therefore, my beloved brethren, be steadfast, immovable, always abounding in the work of the Lord, knowing that your labor is not in vain in the Lord.

1 CORINTHIANS 15:58

But seek first the kingdom of God and His righteousness, and all these things shall be added to you.

MATTHEW 6:33

There are many plans in a man's heart, Nevertheless the LORD's counsel—that will stand.

PROVERBS 19:21

WHEN YOU FEEL
LIKE JOB

If you've ever had a series of setbacks that occurred in your life at the same time, you may have wondered if you would survive it all. The biblical story of Job describes a man who did everything he could to please God, and yet calamity fell on him over and over again. He couldn't understand what was happening.

Some of our "Job" experiences happen for a few days and are gone, but other times, they take us on such a downward spiral that we wonder if recovery is possible. Worse yet, we wonder if God is going to help us get through it. We wonder if God is punishing us or if there is yet hope for the future.

In some very real ways, Job's story is our story. In the end, God gave him even more besides. In the end, He will do the same for us. We can't even imagine what good things He has in store for us in heaven, but we know He's already made plans for our good. Whatever you're going through, remember your Creator. He's the One who has planned a future where there are no tears.

Little Seeds of Hope

"Eye has not seen, nor ear heard,
Nor have entered into the heart of man
The things which God has prepared
for those who love Him."

1 CORINTHIANS 2:9

For the word of the LORD is right,
And all His work is done in truth.
He loves righteousness and justice;
The earth is full of the goodness of the LORD.

PSALM 33:4—5

God, who made the world and everything
in it, since He is Lord of heaven and earth,
does not dwell in temples made with hands.
Nor is He worshiped with men's hands,
as though He needed anything, since He
gives to all life, breath, and all things.

ACTS 17:24—25

FINISH STRONG!

Despite having almost twenty-six miles behind them, marathon runners find a boost of energy when the finish line comes into view. Despite the long hours of labor already behind her, the mother finds the ability to push one more time, and her baby is born. Joy in finishing a long race and achieving a goal can give much-needed strength in a grueling athletic event. Joy over finally being able to meet the child she already loves is a mother's source of strength in the hospital delivery room. Even more, joy in knowing the Lord is a sure source of strength for His people as they face the challenges, hurts, and disappointments of life.

You are undoubtedly bearing a cross of your own. After all, Jesus promised that His people would know trials and tribulations in this world. Yet the joy of the Lord truly can sustain you, whatever you're facing. Stay close to your heavenly Father and know joy despite life's circumstances.

100 Favorite Bible Verses

· · · · · · · · · ·

The joy of the LORD is your strength.

NEHEMIAH 8:10

Do you not know that those who run in a race
all run, but one receives the prize? Run in such
a way that you may obtain it. And everyone
who competes for the prize is temperate in all
things. Now they do it to obtain a perishable
crown, but we for an imperishable crown.

1 CORINTHIANS 9:24—25

Let all those rejoice who put their trust in You;
Let them ever shout for joy,
because You defend them;
Let those also who love Your name
Be joyful in You.

PSALM 5:11

Be glad in the LORD and rejoice, you righteous;
And shout for joy, all you upright in heart!

PSALM 32:11

GIVE YOURSELF AWAY

My heart's desire is to find more opportunities to give myself away and teach my children the joy of service at the same time. One little problem: when?! A friend of mine once moaned, "There's just not enough of me to go around." Lots of us feel the same way and can't bear the thought of adding one more activity, one more "to do" item to our list, however worthy it may be.

For busy women like us, who don't know how we could manage the added role of volunteer, psychologist Virginia O'Leary offers a word of encouragement: "The more roles women have, the better off they are, and the less likely they are to be depressed or discouraged about their lives. When we have a lot to do, we complain that it's driving us crazy—but, in fact, it's what keeps us sane."

It's ironic that one of the best remedies for impending burnout is to give yourself away. To pick one time and place each week where you stretch out your hands for the pure joy of doing it.

LIZ CURTIS HIGGS

Only Angels Can Wing It

By this we know love, because He laid down His life for us. And we also ought to lay down our lives for the brethren. But whoever has this world's goods, and sees his brother in need, and shuts up his heart from him, how does the love of God abide in him?

1 JOHN 3:16—17

"Whoever receives one little child like this in My name receives Me."

MATTHEW 18:5

"'Lord, when did we see You hungry and feed You, or thirsty and give You drink? When did we see You a stranger and take You in, or naked and clothe You? Or when did we see You sick, or in prison, and come to You?' And the King will answer and say to them, 'Assuredly, I say to you, inasmuch as you did it to one of the least of these My brethren, you did it to Me.'"

MATTHEW 25:37—40

WHAT DOES GOD SEE?

When I met my husband, Dave, I liked him. As I spent time with him, I got to know him more and more. We talked, laughed, and even cried together, and I realized my "like" had turned into love, and I couldn't get enough of him.

When God surveys our love for Him, I wonder what He sees. Does He find us being in "like" with Him only? Is He sorrowful for what He knows our relationship could be but isn't because of the absence of time together? Is He sad when we talk and laugh and cry only with others? Does He weep when we let the fire of our love grow cold?

Falling in love with God happens through time spent. The more time we spend with Him, the more we fall in love. It's that simple. It's that joyous. It's that wonderful.

LYNDA HUNTER BJORKLUND

Women of Faith Devotional Bible

What does the LORD your God require of you,
but to fear the LORD your God, to walk in all His
ways and to love Him, to serve the LORD your
God with all your heart and with all your soul?

DEUTERONOMY 10:12

I am persuaded that neither death nor life,
nor angels nor principalities nor powers,
nor things present nor things to come, nor
height nor depth, nor any other created thing,
shall be able to separate us from the love of
God which is in Christ Jesus our Lord.

ROMANS 8:38—39

We love Him because He first loved us.

1 JOHN 4:19

ROLLER COASTERS

For each of us, life can feel like a roller coaster. One minute you're heading toward the top of the highest peak, somewhat apprehensive but excited. The next minute you're heading downward faster than you ever thought you'd go, and you're not sure if you're screaming with sheer terror or joy. What do you do? You hold on! You hold on to the hope that God always has for you.

Your roller-coaster experience may be about crashing financial pictures, or about the unexpected death of someone you love, or about your spouse being deployed to a volatile part of the world. Personal tragedies abound, and somehow between the ones we experience ourselves and the ones we hear about from our friends, we're overwhelmed with those tragedies. We can hardly catch our breath before another one hits us. It's definitely not an easy ride.

How do we smooth things out and hold on? We find an anchor. God gave us His Son and His Spirit to comfort us and strengthen us. He knows we'll hit hard times along with the good times, and so He never leaves us alone.

Little Seeds of Hope

For You are my hope, O Lord GOD;
You are my trust from my youth.
By You I have been upheld from birth;
You are He who took me out of my mother's womb.
My praise shall be continually of You.

PSALM 71:5–6

God is our refuge and strength,
A very present help in trouble.
Therefore we will not fear,
Even though the earth be removed,
And though the mountains be carried
into the midst of the sea;
Though its waters roar and be troubled,
Though the mountains shake with its swelling.

PSALM 46:1–3

Now may the God of hope fill you with all joy
and peace in believing, that you may abound
in hope by the power of the Holy Spirit.

ROMANS 15:13

HOPE IN THE
LORD, NOT MAN

Be sure that your future hope is firmly rooted *only* in the one true God.

Loving fellowship with people and placing trust in them is a relational gift ordained by God, but it should never replace our need for God. On this point the apostle Paul wrote, "We . . . comfort those who are in any affliction, with the comfort with which we ourselves are comforted by God" (2 Corinthians 1:4–5). It is helpful to remember that when friends let you down—and it will happen, at some point, to everyone—you will find it easier to forgive and move forward if your trust is secure in the immovable, unchangeable love of the Savior.

While You can't know for certain that your friends will be faithful and loyal when you need them most, you *can* know that God will fill that expectation! Resolve today to be a friend who loves with a Christlike love, but seek your deepest soul-comfort in the one true Source. *He* will never let you down.

A Jane Austen Devotional

Oh, taste and see that the LORD is good;
Blessed is the man who trusts in Him!

PSALM 34:8

Through the LORD's mercies we are not consumed,
Because His compassions fail not.
They are new every morning;
Great is Your faithfulness.

LAMENTATIONS 3:22—23

He Himself has said, "I will never
leave you nor forsake you."

HEBREWS 13:5

FRIENDS FOR
ALL SEASONS

If family is the way we establish our roots on earth's soil, then friends are the fertilizer. Friends are the sunshine and the rain, the ones who help us grow to be better and stronger than we'd be on our own. In that regard we cultivate a variety of types of friends.

Some friends are part of our work environment, and they bring us insight into the projects at hand or the opportunities around us. They nurture our desires to become better at the things we do. They encourage our growth along the path of our career choices.

If we're truly blessed, there's a friend or two who creates a space for us like no one else can do. They help us to dig deeper into who we are and what we want out of life. They nourish our spirits with laughter and warm conversations each time we meet. They are the gifts that truly strengthen our growth and help us become beautiful.

These friends are with you when hope is thin, the ones who remind you brighter days are just ahead and that God is with you. This kind of friendship is rooted in love.

Little Seeds of Hope

A friend loves at all times,
And a brother is born for adversity.

PROVERBS 17:17

A man who has friends must himself be friendly,
But there is a friend who sticks
closer than a brother.

PROVERBS 18:24

Do not forsake your own friend
or your father's friend.

PROVERBS 27:10

PUT OFF
PROCRASTINATION

Do you have pet procrastinations? Maybe you want to lose five pounds but you keep putting off that daily three-mile walk you pledged to yourself in order to help that happen. Maybe you want to go back to college, but you always find it too difficult to get the application filled out. Timing is everything, and so if you're missing the boat too often, you may want to rethink your priorities and let God help you set some new goals.

You know you're willing to put off things that don't really appeal to you. You've been planning to read the Bible more or to pray more regularly. What if today was all you had left? Do the things today that would mean the most to you, and discover what to make a priority.

Give yourself credit today for each choice you make to complete something you started, stick to a plan you created, or not give yourself an out to put something off. Give God thanks for this day and the opportunity you have to start again to do things right.

Your Promises from God Today

He who observes the wind will not sow,
And he who regards the clouds will not reap.

ECCLESIASTES 11:4

To everything there is a season,
A time for every purpose under heaven:
A time to be born,
And a time to die;
A time to plant,
And a time to pluck what is planted;
A time to kill,
And a time to heal;
A time to break down,
And a time to build up.

ECCLESIASTES 3:1–3

The LORD will perfect that which concerns me;
Your mercy, O LORD, endures forever;
Do not forsake the works of Your hands.

PSALM 138:8

SET FREE FROM SIN

Why does our hair do that? You know, how it frizzes, frays, and frustrates as it flies around in the salty breeze. . . .

Salt-air hair can remind us of this truth [from today's verse]: there are just some things that are out of our control . . . and . . . cannot succeed against God. . . .

Times when evil seems to win: . . . our best friend is making a wrong decision, we give in to an addiction we think we've long ago conquered . . . We want to retaliate. . . . Since God instructs us to let Him take care of these matters, our own schemes really won't work. In due time, either now or in the final tally, those who have wronged us will have to answer to God as well. He is fair like that.

So celebrate this truth. . . . Let your hair fly free as a reminder that your soul already does.

MIRIAM DRENNAN

Devotions for the Beach

. . . .

There is no wisdom, no insight, no plan
that can succeed against the Lord.

PROVERBS 21:30 NIV

A man's heart plans his way,
But the Lord directs his steps.

PROVERBS 16:9

Now having been set free from sin, and having
become slaves of God, you have your fruit to
holiness, and the end, everlasting life. For
the wages of sin is death, but the gift of God
is eternal life in Christ Jesus our Lord.

ROMANS 6:22—23

DIVINE APPOINTMENTS

About a year ago we had a second phone line installed in our home that was only one digit off from the long distance information line in a certain region of South Carolina. At first I was so frustrated with the influx of callers wanting phone numbers to Bud's Seafood and Bessie's Best Bathing Suit Shop. Just as I was about to call the phone company and demand they fix the problem immediately, God reminded me of my commitment to make the most of every evangelism opportunity He gives me.

So the "God line" was born. I started proudly answering the phone, "God-line information. We don't have all the answers but we know the One who does. How may I help you?" Most of the time I get a bewildered "Huh?" on the other line, but every now and then God uses this wrong number to set divine appointments with Him.

LYSA TERKEURST

Living Life on Purpose

· · · · · · · · · ·

May the LORD repay every man
for his righteousness and his faithfulness.

1 SAMUEL 26:23

My eyes shall be on the faithful of the land,
That they may dwell with me;
He who walks in a perfect way,
He shall serve me.

PSALM 101:6

"His lord said to him, 'Well done, good and
faithful servant; you were faithful over a
few things, I will make you ruler over many
things. Enter into the joy of your lord.'"

MATTHEW 25:21

OPENING THE DOOR
OF HOSPITALITY

Everything I needed to know about being hospitable I learned from Lois the first evening she invited me to dinner in her home. . . . When I arrived, she opened the door and warmly invited me in. I followed her to the kitchen where, to be frank, I expected to see the preparation of an elaborate meal. Lois's husband was a doctor and, to be perfectly honest, that raised my expectations. I saw nothing. I smelled nothing. As I began to wonder about this meal, she opened the refrigerator door and casually asked, "Let's see, what shall we have for dinner?" She wasn't kidding! Before long I had joined her search for food and her creative approach to preparation. Then we began cooking it together. Inwardly I breathed a big sigh of relief. Even I can do this, I thought.

After experiencing this comfortable approach, not only did I know I could do this, but my heart desired to do it. When our hospitality emphasizes pleasing people rather than elaborately preparing for them, much of the stress evaporates.

CHRISTINE WOOD

Character Witness

Above all things have fervent love for one another, for "love will cover a multitude of sins." Be hospitable to one another without grumbling. As each one has received a gift, minister it to one another, as good stewards of the manifold grace of God.

1 PETER 4:8—10

"The righteous will answer Him, saying, 'Lord, when did we see You hungry and feed You, or thirsty and give You drink? When did we see You a stranger and take You in, or naked and clothe You? Or when did we see You sick, or in prison, and come to You?' And the King will answer and say to them, 'Assuredly, I say to you, inasmuch as you did it to one of the least of these My brethren, you did it to Me.'"

MATTHEW 25:37—40

Be kindly affectionate to one another with brotherly love, in honor giving preference to one another; . . . distributing to the needs of the saints, given to hospitality.

ROMANS 12:10, 13

TIME TO REST

Times change, but our basic needs remain stable. We need rest. You should see my neighbor. While I rush through one job with my mind on the next in line, she just drops down on the grass, idly chewing a pepperwood stem. "I'm unable to finish all that needs doing today, so what's the rush?" [and] "I accomplish more if I sit a spell—not working—just thinking and appreciating." . . .

Somewhere there's a recipe for people like me who try to do a year's work in one day—and rob themselves of "thinking time." My friend reads "so I can know the hopes and dreams in a world before my time," she says. My friend listens to music "so I can enlarge my heart and mind." My friend prays "so I can enlarge my soul." Her philosophy is contagious.

JUNE MASTERS BACHER

Quiet Moments for Women

In Your presence is fullness of joy;
At Your right hand are pleasures forevermore.

PSALM 16:11

The eyes of the LORD are on the righteous,
And His ears are open to their prayers.

1 PETER 3:12

I set my face toward the Lord God to make
request by prayer. . . . I prayed to the LORD
my God, and made confession, and said, "O
Lord, great and awesome God, who keeps His
covenant and mercy with those who love Him,
and with those who keep His commandments."

DANIEL 9:3–4

A DISCIPLINED
PRAYER LIFE

The value of time spent in prayer cannot be overestimated.

Jesus offered a striking example of regular prayer. Throughout His ministry, Jesus would "withdraw to desolate places and pray" (Luke 5:16). Jesus' apostles followed His lead, and now, as Christ followers twenty centuries later, we are encouraged to do the same. The many benefits of prayer include communing with God, learning to listen for His voice, and letting His words and thoughts guide our lives. Think of that! *We have a direct means of communicating with God*. When we pray, we speak the unique language of our relationship with Him.

If you desire to be a true disciple of Christ—if you want to become like Him—there is no better place to start than with consistent times of devoted prayer.

A Jane Austen Devotional

Now it came to pass, as He was praying in a certain place, when He ceased, that one of His disciples said to Him, "Lord, teach us to pray, as John also taught his disciples."

LUKE 11:1

Now when Daniel knew that the writing [that forbade worship of anyone other than the king] was signed, he went home. And in his upper room, with his windows open toward Jerusalem, he knelt down on his knees three times that day, and prayed and gave thanks before his God, as was his custom since early days. Then these men assembled and found Daniel praying and making supplication before his God.

DANIEL 6:10—11

PURPOSEFUL PAIN

Wander by an old dock or around some boat slips, and you'll hear the muffled, rhythmic moans of ropes, indicative of pain, of tension, of the purposeful intent to hang on. . . .

Now move in closer and study those ropes. You'll notice that time and tension also contributed to their frayed, discolored appearance. Ironically, however, these alleged blemishes make them more pliable, more useful, and even stronger. . . .

How many days do you experience something similar? You are quietly straining, moaning, painfully trying to keep it together for the sake of others, and maybe unsure that you can. . . . You bear the marks of time and experience, but don't seem to gain the wisdom and strength.

Quite often, our pain has purpose, but just as often, we don't see it. Instead, we focus on the fear of what might happen if our grip should slip.

The difference is, however, that even if we let go, God hasn't let go of us. He doesn't. And He won't.

MIRIAM DRENNAN

Devotions for the Beach

198

· · · · · · · · ·

The pain turned you to God.

2 CORINTHIANS 7:9 TLB

In this you greatly rejoice, though now for a little while, if need be, you have been grieved by various trials, that the genuineness of your faith, being much more precious than gold that perishes, though it is tested by fire, may be found to praise, honor, and glory at the revelation of Jesus Christ.

1 PETER 1:6—7

Count it all joy when you fall into various trials, knowing that the testing of your faith produces patience. But let patience have its perfect work, that you may be perfect and complete, lacking nothing.

JAMES 1:2—4

SEEDS OF JOY

It's human nature to notice red lights, lines that are moving faster than yours, and dogs that behave better than yours. This tendency doesn't make it easy to find joy in the day-to-day aspects of life. It instead keeps us focused on ourselves and on how unfair life can be.

But we don't have to live like that. We can learn to obey the command of Philippians 4:4, "Rejoice in the Lord always. Again I will say, rejoice!" We can learn to rejoice—always! Note that Paul didn't say to rejoice about your circumstances. He didn't call us to celebrate hurtful relationships or painful losses. Speaking on God's behalf, Paul instead commanded us to rejoice in the Lord—in His sovereign power, His unwavering goodness, and His unfailing love.

So train yourself to look for evidence of God's presence and activity in your life. Let people know when [you are] very aware of God being at work in your life.

Be warned! These seeds of joy that you sow will bear the fruit of more joy!

100 Favorite Bible Verses

Most of all, friends, always rejoice in the
Lord! I never tire of saying it: Rejoice!
PHILIPPIANS 4:4 THE VOICE

Be glad in the LORD and rejoice, you righteous;
And shout for joy, all you upright in heart!
PSALM 32:11

Your mercy, O LORD, is in the heavens;
Your faithfulness reaches to the clouds.
PSALM 36:5

Forever, O LORD,
Your word is settled in heaven.
Your faithfulness endures to all generations.
PSALM 119:89—90

ACKNOWLEDGMENTS

Grateful acknowledgment is made to the following authors and publishers for permission to reprint copyrighted material.

100 Favorite Bible Verses. Thomas Nelson, 2011.

Bacher, June Masters. *The Quiet Heart: Daily Devotionals for Women.* Harvest House, 1988.

Bacher, June Masters. *Quiet Moments for Women.* Harvest House, 1979.

Barnhill, Julie Ann. *Exquisite Hope.* Tyndale, 2005.

Barnhill, Julie Ann. *Scandalous Grace.* Tyndale, 2003.

Bateman, Lana, Lynda Hunter Bjorklund, Dee Brestin, Cynthia Heald, Nicole Johnson, Denise Jones, Babbie Mason, Heather Mercer, Sara Trollinger, Luci Swindoll. *Women of Faith Devotional Bible: A Message of Grace & Hope for Every Day.* Thomas Nelson, 2003.

Demoss, Nancy Leigh. *Lies Women Believe: And the Truth that Sets Them Free.* Moody Publishers, 2006.

Drennan, Miriam. *Devotions for the Beach . . . and Days You Wish You Were There.* Thomas Nelson, 2012.

Elliot, Elisabeth. *Keep a Quiet Heart.* Revell, 2004. elisabethelliot.org.

Elliot, Elisabeth. *On Asking God Why: And Other Reflections on Trusting God in a Twisted World.* Revell, 2006.

Elliot, Elisabeth. *A Path Through Suffering: Discovering the Relationship Between God's Mercy and Our Pain.* Regal, 2003. elisabethelliot.org.

Elliot, Elisabeth. *The Shaping of a Christian Family: How My Parents Nurtured My Faith.* Revell, 2005. elisabethelliot.org.

Gaither, Gloria. *Decisions: A Christian's Approach to Making Right Choices.* Word Books, 1982. Copyright © 1982 Gloria Gaither. All rights reserved. Used by permission.

Hale, Mandy. *The Single Woman: Life, Love, and a Dash of Sass.* Thomas Nelson, 2013.

Harper, Lisa. *Stumbling into Grace: Confessions of a Sometimes Spiritually Clumsy Woman.* Thomas Nelson, 2011.

Higgs, Liz Curtis. *Only Angels Can Wing It: The Rest of Us Have to Practice.* Thomas Nelson, 1995.

A Jane Austen Devotional. Thomas Nelson, 2012.

Little Seeds of Hope. Thomas Nelson, 2013.

Living God's Way: Inspirational Insights for the Path Ahead. Thomas Nelson, 2007.

Lotz, Anne Graham. *I Saw the Lord.* Zondervan, 2007.

More Than a Bucket List. Thomas Nelson, 2012.

Omartian, Stormie. *The Power of a Praying Wife.* Harvest House, 2007.

Omartian, Stormie. *Praying God's Will for Your Life.* Thomas Nelson, 2001.

Parsons, Marian (Miss Mustard Seed). *Inspired You: Breathing New Life into Your Heart and Home.* Thomas Nelson, 2012.

Pearcey, Nancy. *Total Truth: Liberating Christianity from Its Cultural Captivity.* © 2004. Used by permission of Crossway, a publishing ministry of Good News Publishers, Wheaton, IL 60187, www.crossway.org.

Renfroe, Anita. *The Purse-Driven Life: It Really Is All About Me.* Copyright © 2005. Used by permission of NavPress, All Rights Reserved. www.navpress.com (1-800-366-7788).

Tada, Joni Eareckson. *Seeking God: My Journey of Prayer and Praise.* Wolgemuth & Hyatt, 1991.

TerKeurst, Lysa. *Living Life on Purpose: Discovering God's Best for Your Life.* Moody, 2000.

Trobisch, Ingrid. *The Hidden Strength: Rooted in the Security of God's Love.* Thomas Nelson, 1988.

Wood, Christine. *Character Witness: How Our Lives Can Make a Difference in Evangelism.* IVP Books, 2003.

Yates, Susan Alexander. *A House Full of Friends: How to Like the Ones You Love.* Focus on the Family, 1995.

Your Promises from God Today. Thomas Nelson, 2013.